MW01165423

Modeling From the Ground Up

Strategies for Building a Successful Modeling Career

JEANNE REJAUNIER

Copyright 2012 © Jeanne Rejaunier

All rights reserved.

ISBN: 10: 147824254X
ISBN- 13: 978-1478242543

CONTENTS

Preface

Chapter 1 -Starting Out in Modeling

Chapter 2 - Testing, Training and Model Selling Tools

Chapter 3 - Rounds, Seeing Clients, and Marketing Yoursef

Chapter 4 - Categories and Casting Breakdowns

Chapter 5 - A Model Needs to Know

Chapter 6 - Modeling Niches

Chapter 7 - Makeup and Hairstyling

Chapter 8- Working with Photographers

Chapter 9 - Markets - USA

Chapter 10 - International Markets

Chapter 11 - Modeling Schools, Pageants, Contests, Scouts

Chapter 12 - Advice to Models

Glossary

About the Author

THE BEAUTY TRAP, by Jeanne Rejaunier

JEANNE REJAUNIER

PREFACE

When people think of models, the images they most often evoke are of the supermodel/ superstars – those enviably thin, beautiful, famous and highly paid young women, as well as their male counterparts – towering, gorgeous, hunky men. Out of tens of thousands of models across the globe, the hype centers around a select few who are seen in fashion spreads, print ads, TV commercials, and elite runway appearances at glittering fashion capitals of the world. High powered mannequins enjoy lucrative beauty and fashion contracts worth millions of dollars. They are constantly in the public eye, written and talked about by the media and P.R. people. But these are not the only kind of models. The fact is, armed with a set of professional photos, together with enough resolve, ambition and stamina, many other types can also be models.

Modeling is a rewarding and extraordinarily well paying field in which a demand exists for every type, age, sex, coloring and ethnicity. Some models are bald, fat men; some are older women, some are infants and children. Some models are large, plus size, others petites. Some are elderly. Some, "parts models" model only portions of themselves – hands, legs, feet, feet.

The kind of work a model is hired to do reaches across a wide spectrum: print, including catalog, product advertising, publicity, fashion editorial, beauty and glamour; television commercial, video and industrial; runway, retail, wholesale; convention, live demonstration, live industrial – even some acting assignments sometimes fall loosely under the category of "modeling" and are often performed by models.

Younger models with the qualifications to make it in fashion and beauty have their future carved out. If you are a young woman of energy and drive with the height, facial planes and potential for working in front of a camera, there is virtually no limit to what you can achieve. And even if you are no raving beauty, there can be a place for you as a "real person" model. Happily for those who are performers rather than mannequins and are considered "talent," unlike fashion and beauty types, you have no problem with "aging out." Know that yours can be a career of limitless sights over decades in time.

Modeling is a very large international industry, in which European and regional US agencies and clients play a big part, with New York at its summit. Modeling has always been competitive, but today is even more so. There is no one path to achieve modeling fame and fortune; but certain factors are constants.

In assessing your potential, you should determine the needs of the industry balanced with your look and abilities. As you read further into this book, you will see what you need to do to highlight your uniqueness, find an agent and get work. You will discover pointers on building your portfolio, how to style your promotional tools, and find insights on other techniques to help you arrive at modeling success.

CHAPTER 1 - STARTING OUT IN MODELING

So you want to be a model?

Do you want to model, or are you being pushed toward modeling by friends and family? With the huge media hype given models, mothers worldwide are eager for their offspring, usually daughters, to model; even boyfriends and girlfriends seek to bask in reflected glory. It's not uncommon to be attracted to the glitz and glitter surrounding modeling. But to be a successful model, you yourself must want it. It takes dedication and the will to work hard to make it in this enormously competitive industry.

What do you know about modeling? Perhaps you have your own model fantasies. Do you covet the glamour of three day shoots in the Mediterranean or the Caribbean – flying all over the world from city to city ... Vogue and Harper's Bazaar layouts, swimsuit calendars, posters and Sports Illustrated covers ... exclusive Calvin Klein, Victoria's Secret and Revlon contracts paying in the seven figures per year ... designer shows, catalog work, TV commercials, maybe even Hollywood offers?

Some of the above are reachable goals for so-called supermodels, and possibly for other types as well – within limits. For modeling is a field that depends upon type; you can't be something you're not, and major disappointment can be avoided once a fledgling model takes stock and realizes exactly how she/he sizes up in the area of modeling he or she is aiming for. If there is a demand for your type, or if you can create that demand, if modeling is what you really want, and you're willing to work hard, then definitely go for it.

Modeling can be a tremendous career enabling world travel, an über-chic lifestyle, and making incredible amounts of money. As never before, models today are sought after as symbols and icons; they have unprecedented glamour, independence, and freedom;

they are at the center of things. No wonder so many people want to be models. For modeling can offer:

– Fame and recognition
– Financial rewards
– Adventure, accomplishment, independence
– A launching pad for allied fields
– Glamorous lifestyle, meeting interesting people

Through modeling, you can maximize your talents, embellish your interest in fashion, clothing, hairstyles and makeup, and open doors to opportunities not to be found anywhere else. All of this can be compelling reasons for entering the profession. But to make it in the modeling industry, you must be motivated and a self-starter. Remember, it's never enough to have other people tell you "you should model." Modeling demands discipline in which professionalism is expected. You must give your all to a modeling career or you won't amount to much. A pretty face can be the very least requirement, and often it's not the most beautiful girl or the handsomest guy who makes it in modeling.

Do you have what legendary Elite Model Agency founder John Casablancas called "that killer thing"? Modeling requires not only more than looks but more than talent. It takes perseverance and a desire and willingness to constantly learn and improve yourself. You can't be someone who discourages easily. You must be able to withstand criticism and rejection, weather setbacks and continue despite disappointment and failure. Every day you will have to get out and push, ring bells, knock on doors, make people aware of who you are, and refuse to take no for an answer. You must be thick skinned. You have to truly want modeling with a burning desire.

The modeling work is there, waiting to be filled. The sky's the limit, providing you prove to the powers that be that you're a reliable hard worker, serious about growing and improving as a model. Even if you don't become one of the industry's top earners in the seven and eight figure a year category, it's definitely possible to earn a consistently tidy amount over several years if you make the right moves. Steps up the ladder can become giant leaps, dependent upon expert management, lucky breaks, and your own tireless efforts.

Is there an ideal age and size for modeling?

Female fashion models are restricted in age and size. Ideally, they should be under 22 years old when they begin, preferably still teenagers. They must be tall – at least 5' 8, preferably more, 5' 9 to 5' 11 being the ideal height. 6' to 6' 2 is the height requirement for male fashion models, though some exceptions can be made for either sex in some markets. Fashion modeling for women, whether editorial, catalog, or runway, is a career of limited duration, usually less than ten years, supermodels and celebrity models sometimes excepted. Male fashion models can start later and continue longer.

For other areas of modeling, especially commercials and advertising print, any age, size and shape will do, according to the market and specific assignment. Since modeling uses all types, for many there is no ideal age. Some models can continue for decades, as long as they maintain a marketable look. TV commercial and commercial print models can be any age, size, or sex, whether gay, straight, black, white, yellow, red or shades in between. They can be kids, character people, uglies, even weirdos.

As for the best age to begin modeling, the sooner the better is a good idea, meaning it's never too soon. Many top movie stars started modeling as infants and young children, persevered over the years, and were pros in the business before they were old enough to drive. However, by the same token, many successful models have begun careers later on, particularly men and character or "real people" types.

What do you need to start?

You need an agent. A model agency's belief in the model is a model's major foundational given. Without an agency behind her or him, a model is severely handicapped. Every model, no matter how much initiative he/she has, needs the push only expert management can give. Even the best self-starter in the business must have a support system to maximize a successful career.

An agent who believes a model has the potential to be a major star won't stop until stardom is a fait accompli. The agent presents the model to those in a position to hire, pre-sells and post-sells, instructs, shapes, coaches, and cheers a model on from the sidelines. Look and you will always find a mentor behind the superstars. Be it great model agency legends like Eileen Ford, John Casablancas, Monique Pillard, David Bosman, Frances Grill, a model maven in a US secondary market or in one of the European capitals, you will always find someone who sold, pushed and overcame any and all odds to make the magic happen, who became the secret weapon in the model's success.

Added to that, you will usually discover that there is another key person in the industry who nodded assent to make the big break occur – a photographer, editor, designer, cosmetics company or other high profile client. The model more than anyone relies on others to open doors and provide the breaks that push him to the forefront.

Timing is a definite factor – being at the right place at the right time with the right look. If you are lucky enough to meet the very clients who are seeking someone exactly like you, if your appearance in their lives should coincide with a high profile spot being cast, and you are offered the golden opportunity that focuses attention on you, you're on your way.

This attention need not be instant world-wide recognition; industry insider recognition is enough to pave the way to build for better things to come. At whatever stage you are, if you stand out from the crowd, make a vivid impression to the right people, you will start the ball rolling, a groundswell will occur leading to the next step – and so on and on.

A modeling career can be initiated different ways, ranging from discovery at conventions, contests and pageants, regional experience and other channels. Agencies run contests (Ford and Elite: Look of the Year, Supermodel of the World, America's Next Supermodel, etc.). Some agencies employ model scouts on a salaried basis, others use scouts to whom they give a percentage of the model's earnings. Some scouts prowl outside contests, conventions, pageants, and modeling schools, some advertise in the newspaper or conduct seminars locally, looking to attract new faces.

Models are spotted in public at a mall, concert or sporting event. Some are stopped on escalators in busy department stores and in other populated locations. Some literally walk in off the street, others pick up a phone, ring an agency they find listed online or in the yellow pages, request an appointment, are interviewed, accepted, and start right in testing with photographers, pounding the pavements, making rounds.

And of course, the majority of agencies hold interviews in which anyone can stop by and fill out an application. Most agencies have open interviews one or two days a week devoted to seeing new people. This is true of agencies in the major cities of New York, Los Angeles, Chicago, and Miami, as well as smaller markets like Boston, Philadelphia, Seattle, the Carolinas, and others. Depending on agency requirements, aspiring models may be expected to send pictures ahead before scheduling an appointment. Some agencies want to see a Polaroid or a collection of snapshots first, and will get in touch with the model only if they are interested.

What's the best city for modeling?

The major international modeling markets, offering the most work, money and prestige are New York, Paris, London, Milan, Tokyo. Secondary American markets in which models can also find plentiful work are Los Angeles, Miami and Chicago.

Also in the United States, Boston, Philadelphia, Dallas, Houston, Atlanta, Arizona, San Francisco, Seattle, Orlando, Tampa,

Cleveland, Detroit, New Orleans, and the Carolinas are smaller markets but not to be overlooked, as they are very good to gain experience in. Other markets are found in countless less populated US cities that also offer good work to models.

Secondary foreign markets offering work opportunities to models include Toronto, Sydney, Hamburg, Munich, Rome, Florence, Barcelona, Madrid, Tel Aviv, Zurich, Vienna, Montreal, Athens, Osaka, and others.

A model may begin work in virtually any of the above cities, or in others not mentioned. There is nothing to stop a model from launching a career in Pittsburgh, Oklahoma City, Austin, Oshkosh – or anywhere in the world.

In Chapters 9 and 10 we will cover these cities in greater detail.

Will moving to New York increase a model's chances for success?

At one time, it was a foregone conclusion that because New York City is the modeling capital of the world, those serious about making it in modeling should always be based there. While the Big Apple indeed continues to be modeling's pinnacle, less and less is New York the ideal place from which to launch a career, due to the tremendous amount of competition.

That's not to say that each year, many new faces don't begin in New York and find, by degrees, eventual success. However, today more than ever before, it is recommended that models get some experience prior to trying their luck in the most competitive market of all – so the conventional wisdom is that in the beginning, models should initially stick closer to home in a secondary market.

Most New York-based models are originally from elsewhere, having begun in local U.S. markets or Europe. Though it is wise to have previous modeling experience before tackling Manhattan, if you are a native New Yorker (that is, hailing from the tri-state New

York/New Jersey/Connecticut area), know your way around and feel comfortable in the city, you may be able to start from your home base rather than moving to a smaller, slower paced environment.

There is another thing to be said in favor of launching a career in New York. If you are primarily an actor or performer whose secondary career is modeling, you may want to base yourself in New York in order to avail yourself of New York's unparalleled acting teachers, whose reputation, skills and contacts are difficult to find elsewhere in the country. Many New York casting directors also double as TV commercial coaches, which is an added incentive for the actor/performer.

Or perhaps you are a modeling hopeful who lives in or near Chicago, Dallas, Houston, Miami, Tampa, Toronto, Atlanta, Los Angeles, or Detroit. Top New York agencies have representatives or branches in these and other major cities who will give you an interview right where you are. After you've worked in your market for a while, your agency may feed you to their counterpart in New York.

Some new faces make trips abroad to hopefully accomplish in less time in Europe what would take much longer to do in New York, and this may be another option you would like to pursue. Secondary markets as well as international modeling will be discussed in later chapters.

How many model agencies in the world are there?

An educated guess is several thousand. In New York alone there are hundreds. Los Angeles, counting talent agencies, comes close to that figure; Paris has a hundred or more agencies. When you start adding up all the agencies from the major and secondary markets, the number can easily reach an astounding five figure number – and growing.

What kind of work do agencies offer models?

Model agencies themselves do not offer models work, but find work for them by sending the model to potential clients who book them for jobs. The majority of modeling jobs are in fashion, and are for women. Some models specialize in one area alone, others in two or more. Basic modeling areas include:

– Print modeling: fashion editorial - photos in magazines; catalog; commercial advertising - national upscale advertising, billboards, newspapers, public relations.

 – Film and tape: television commercials, music videos and filmed industrial shows.

– Live modeling - promotional and product demonstration; convention modeling, hostessing, live industrials, trade shows, conventions, live promotional.

– Wholesale and retail modeling: designer or manufacturer's showroom modeling - in house modeling; fit modeling

– Informal floor modeling - in department stores, restaurants, tearooms, mingling with customers.

– Runway modeling - for designer collections, trunk shows, or retail in department stores.

A variety of types are used in the above categories, each with different requirements being emphasized. Some criteria further defined:

– If a model is employed by a designer as a fit model, she must be a sample size and maintain her weight.

– A runway model must move gracefully and look current. Runway models must know how to show garments to advantage.

– A promotional model's look may be business professional, all-

American/girl next door, or glamour type. For male promo models, the type most in demand is businessman.

Other modeling jobs demand special skills, such as acting, singing, dancing, tennis, swimming, driving a car, golf, or horseback riding, etc.

Sometimes an outstanding physical feature will help a model get the job – a great body, thick eyelashes, a small waistline. Personality, charisma and animation are always pluses for a model of any type and category.

All types and categories are needed, including:

– High fashion models - appearing in magazines such as Vogue, Harper's Bazaar, etc.; on runways modeling designer collections; in catalogs, commercials and print advertising for high profile, prestige products; these models usually have a sophisticated, elegant look; some are exotic, others more commercial; some combine the two; most fashion models are 5'9 to 5'11, ages 15-25 (some exceptions).

– General fashion - pretty all-American, contemporary woman, late 20's to mid 40's; "classic woman," over 45.

– Junior models - teens, Seventeen magazine types, can be shorter than high fashion, 5'6 to 5'8".

– Plus models - large women, wearing clothes size 14 on up, often 18 up.

– Petites - wear sizes 1-7, are 5'2-5-6; under age 25

– Male fashion models - GQ type, appears on runways worldwide, usually age 21-35, though can even be 60 and older if the right type; appear solo or paired with women in ads and fashion spreads.

– General fashion males: can be any age, but are usually under 45; can be 18 for college look, 25-35 for young father and business executive; appear in a range of clothing – formal, business, casual, underwear, swimwear; big and tall male models are 44 longs and up.

– Infants and children - all ages and types

– Product models - all ages and types

– TV commercial models - all types: some are real people models, character and specialty models; commercial models may overlap with all other types.

– Parts modeling - models hands, legs, feet. Legs must be smooth, hairless, impeccably groomed; small feet are in demand and must be well cared for; no calluses or blemishes, pretty toenails.

Casting breakdowns

– Infants and children – all ages, newborns on up
– Teens – 13-19
– College kids – 17-22
– Girl next door – 18-25
– Young adult – 22-25
– Young mother – 21- 35
– Homemaker – 28-45
– Businesswoman – 28-55
– Glamour girl – 20 - 32   (can be older if celebrity model)
– Young father – 24-35
– Older father – 30-50
– Husband – 28-45
– Businessman – 30-60
– Retiree – 55 up
– Grandparents – over 50
– Spokespeople – usually over 30

Modeling is an image business

A model's physical presentation is his calling card. Modeling is a business based on type and quality. As it has been said, you can't be something you're not – but you can make the most of what you are, either by highlighting and emphasizing, or minimizing and camouflaging. There are many approaches to both, and part of being a pro is learning to play with those approaches.

As a model, you must get used to seeing yourself from countless angles in a myriad of different situations.

How does a model get work?

To emphasize again, to be taken seriously as a model you will ideally first need an agent – although models in some categories do work without one, but it is not the best idea. You will need photos, a book (model's portfolio), test shots and duplicate photos for circulation to clients.

Once you have representation, you're ready to start testing, building your book and going out on rounds, that is, calling on those in a position to book you – photographers, editors, casting directors, production and advertising agency people, depending on where your career focus lies, where your agency chooses to direct you and what type of work is currently available in your market.

Are agencies looking for new models?

Agencies never stop recruiting. A potential model will find model agencies are always available for a look see. Agencies can't exist without models and clients are always seeking new faces.

What type of agency is best?

Agencies may range from small boutique operations to large multi-service companies that specialize in everything – print, runway, TV, plus models, petites, parts modeling, classics (older women), children – to agencies that do print exclusively or commercials exclusively, and so on. One size does not fit all. There is no one answer to what kind of agency is best for a model. The decision of whom to model with is an individual one – a combination of where your focus lies, what area(s) you will be concentrating on, and your type. If you are not only a model but acting talent, you will want to become acquainted with as many talent agencies as possible to decide which is the best match for you.

How long can a modeling career last?

A fashion model's career generally spans a five to ten year range, except in unusual circumstances. Male fashion models last longer. Forty is a great age for a man, and many men are still on the runways past 50 or more, depending on their look.

Many supermodels today are now well into their 40's, 50's, 60's and more. These women have used modeling to branch out into other areas – acting, design and manufacturing, writing, lecturing. To keep going past one decade, most models must become established as celebrities.

Real people models and character actors need not worry about time limits. Real people/ character people will never lack for demand, as long as they maintain a marketable look as they age. Children who stay in the business can have long careers and grow into other types, as they mature. Children and character people have a distinct advantage, in that due to their longevity, they tend to grow on the powers that be, who will come to see them as old friends whose work they respect and whom they continue to want to work with.

What look is best?

An identifiable, marketable look is the most important physical requirement for a model. It is sometimes difficult to know what look will be in demand what season – it's the waif look one year, the voluptuous look the next. When trends change, models adapt. Notice how legendary supermodel Kate Moss increasingly became less and less waif; as the image that originally brought attention to Kate crested and diminished in popularity, Kate transformed herself and assumed another persona. This is what all models must do, albeit in a less radical manner, each time they step in front of the camera – achieve a metamorphosis, as per requirement of the assignment.

To be a model, you need not be beautiful, you just have to have something that stands out, a quality that people react and respond to favorably. Attitude, clothing, hair and makeup are components of your physical presentation. Proportions count: it's best to be thin boned and tall, with broad shoulders and narrow hips, because the lens distorts the body, making it appear thicker. A fashion model should have good shoulders, a well formed neck and an attractive back.

A top model carries him/herself well, moves with built in rhythm and grace. He/she has a distinctive face with good facial planes and refinement of bone structure. A pleasing profile counts. Bad noses keep 90% of aspirants out.

In some eras (eras coming about every four years in modeling), a model can't look too exotic or too ravishingly beautiful; very often, clients want a glorified girl next door, a face women can identify with. Ethnics, however, are an exception to this rule; their exotic looks have never been a drawback.

Some models may almost pass for average (particularly without their makeup), but still stand out in some way. If you notice models on TV commercials, only a minute percentage are utterly drop dead gorgeous; but they always have something special or unusual about them. Often they are interesting personalities. They create a moment, become a believable character; they react, they interact, and the viewer in turn responds.

Is the ability to project this quality of moving the viewer innate, or can it be learned? Both. It can be brought out in a model but not really taught, even though many classes and workshops exist to develop it. Projection is something the model herself/himself has to either possess naturally, have a feel for, or develop in time through experience.

Other qualities that make or break a model

A model should reflect a positive outlook and possess plenty of energy, because the modeling profession requires tremendous hustling. On camera and off, a model should radiate personality. All popular models have a beautiful smile that naturally creates an aura of warmth and excitement. Personality, experts say, can be over 50% of a model's appeal. Clients want someone who comes alive in front of the lens and projects warmth, excitement and animation. Relaxation and a sense of humor are definite advantages; the model who is comfortable and at ease is valued.

Professionalism, seasoning, and the ability to get the job done are sought after qualities. In an apparent contradiction, a veteran model must still project freshness, and a new face must convince the client that despite a lack of experience, he/she can deliver like a pro.

Shyness can be a serious flaw, unless compensated and overcome: a successful model is someone who genuinely likes people and shows it. Independence, strength, intelligence, courtesy and courage are currently coveted qualities in a woman. Men should appear intriguing, a trifle mysterious, vaguely remote yet very personable.

The model must fit an image, be a specific type, communicate a message, make a firm statement. The look/type must be what the job requires – neither too young nor too old, too commercial if the job is fashion, too geek if the job is businessman, too career woman if the job is junior, and so on. At the same time, a versatile model can switch among categories, display an enormous range and constantly interchange roles. The ability to know what to project and how to assume different looks – glamour, innocent, bitch, sexy, sportive, and so on, are modeling givens.

Being able to handle lines for commercials is also a big plus. The model who takes direction easily has a distinct advantage. Persistence in making rounds and in follow up, focus, and soldiering on in the face of rejection all add up to qualities that make a successful model.

One of the most important qualities in a model is the ability to sell oneself. Some models lack the necessary aggressiveness, while lesser beauties can be successful because of it.

Reliability is demanded of a model, especially in the beginning, when it can be critical to establish yourself as someone who shows up on time, doesn't complain, and gives that extra measure. Admittedly, later on, some entrenched models may unfortunately get a reputation for the opposite of these desirable qualities. Because they have arrived at star status, they are forgiven for a time, but sooner or later their lack of professionalism catches up with them and they are eventually dropped by agencies and clients. Gossip travels so fast in the modeling industry that a reputation can easily be damaged before you know it. So never feel you're above the rest of the pack or that the rules don't apply to you. They apply to everyone who wants to work in the modeling industry.

Almost anyone, i.e. just about everyone could be a model, but each individual must suit the required image, be true to type, work within a range, and hope that the featured category is an in-demand one offering plentiful opportunities for bookings and advancement. Yes, anyone can model in some capacity, if not at the very apex of the modeling world, for a while, but it takes a special quality, hard work and some breaks to get to the top of an opportunity-filled category and last.

Growth of the modeling field in recent years has been phenomenal, and competition is enormous. To forge ahead, you need an agent/mentor with good connections, and in the case of fashion models and perhaps others as well, an agent who can deal with international clients. You must sell your competitive edge. Models today are smarter, better educated, more worldly and sophisticated than ever before, so you must at least match them and always reach beyond and try to do better.

For the majority of hopefuls, modeling can be riddled with rejection, disappointment, and insecurity. Do you have what it takes? Can you deal with the pressures, the drawbacks, the stresses? All these factors weigh in as to whether you will have a good chance at modeling.

If you don't live near a major modeling capital

Try smaller markets, to be discussed in Chapter 9. As modeling has grown by leaps and bounds, even very small cities today have model agencies and modeling outlets through department stores and newspaper advertising. Models from small towns can also look to beauty pageants, model camps, conventions and contests as a career entree. More about these in Chapter 11.

Europe is an important part of a model's career. Going there cold turkey is not the experts' recommended strategy for everyone, though some models have done it successfully. It is usually better to go into a foreign market with the backing of a mother agent. International Modeling will be discussed in Chapter 10 .

Where to find a model agency:

Where does a potential model discover the name of an agency? Most of the world's model agencies are now listed online. Do a search, and you will find a treasure trove of entries. Union franchised model and talent agencies, representing models who are also performers, are listed with the performers' unions – SAG-AFTRA (Screen Actors Guild - American Federation of Television and Radio Artists), Actor's Equity and AGVA (American Guild of Variety Artists) online. You can look in trade publications like Back Stage - Call Sheet, also available online; you may call local advertising agencies, department stores and newspaper fashion pages to ask for recommendations. The Models Mart website sells a directory of model agencies worldwide called THE WORLD

AGENCY LIST which you can order online. For focusing solely on New York agencies, you may buy Models Mart's MODELS BLACK BOOK.

You will want to know you're dealing with a legitimate agency. If needs be, you can check with the Better Business Bureau to see if there are any complaints against an agency you are thinking of aligning with.

How to apply to a model agency:

Interviews are by appointment or through open interview, depending on agency policy. Either call first to find out expected protocol, or check an agency's website, where such information usually appears. Find an agency you wish to pursue and evaluate their stated information and policies online. An inquiry in writing is always acceptable and in many cases advised. Enclose a current photo, Polaroid or snapshot, so the agency can determine your photogenic quality, personality projection, and potential for modeling. If the agency accepts email, attach your photos via this method.

Together with a cover letter, include your resume if you have experience, noting your qualifications and vital statistics, measurements, height, weight, age, coloring; abilities such as dancing, acting, singing, fencing; and anything related that might bolster modeling: ("College fashion board, XYZ department store, Cleveland"), and whether you have been referred by anyone. If you're using snail mail, send your inquiry with a return SASE. Wait for a reply. If a month goes by with no response, follow up with a phone call.

What kind of response can you expect?

You may receive either a written or phone reply, informing you of the degree of agency interest, if any. You may receive a letter or email inviting you to make an appointment, indicating the agency believes you may have potential. If you don't receive an email reply, it's possible the agency is backed up and you may want to try again.

If an agency does not invite you for an interview, you may receive a form letter saying the agency will put your pictures and information on file for possible later use; or you may be rejected outright. If the agency's answer is not what you hoped for, don't give up. You should always try more than one source. Even if you don't immediately connect, you still have a shot at making it in modeling if you persevere. Many successful models were initially rejected by not merely one but several agencies. So do not be daunted. If you believe modeling is for you, keep going.

Your first agency interview:

On an interview, the agency will be studying all aspects of your physical presentation, your coloring, height, weight, style of dress, face and figure, as well as your personality, intelligence, speech, friendliness, and any number of other factors. At the initial interview, the agency will give you their evaluation and tell you whether they want to work with you or not. Agencies in big markets get hundreds of inquiries per week, so if you are applying to one of them, it is unlikely you will be the only model being looked at.

After giving your name to the receptionist, expect to wait outside till you are called. Try not to compare yourself to any of the other hopefuls waiting in the lobby, or to the photos of the faces you see posted on the walls who have had the benefit of the best photography and lighting. Don't feel inadequate. You could easily be the next modeling star. Act like you are.

As your turn arrives, you will be ushered into the office(s) of the prime mover or movers for and interview, in which your potential will be evaluated. You'll be asked a number of questions, such as information regarding age, background, schooling, travel, hobbies, goals, and perhaps also something about your family and lifestyle, particularly if you are a minor.

Yes, no, maybe

If the agency believes you have modeling potential or not, they will advise their degree of interest. This can range from:

– The agency may ask you to sign an exclusive contract
– They may take you on a contingency or trial basis
– They may tell you to come back at a later date
– They may reject you outright.

If an agency can't use you, they will usually give a reason: "We already have your type;" " We don't handle your type;" "We don't feel you're ready to be marketed;" "We would be interested if you would lose weight and change your hair color," or something similar.

If the agency accepts you on an exclusive basis

You will be asked to sign a contract. In this case, you will want to be sure the agency has the ability to provide the kind of service you want and the work for which you are qualified. You should interview with more than one agency, preferably several, before signing with one.

If you are signing union representation (SAG-AFTRA) with an agent, you may want to call the union with specific questions. Union contracts have 90 day out clauses, so that if you are dissatisfied with the agent and fail to make a specified amount of money during the first 90 day time period, you may cancel the contract. It should also be mentioned that usually, if a model or performer is dissatisfied with management at any other time, a mutual agreement to disagree may be arranged.

If you are exclusive with an agency, they will work closely with you to establish a look, obtain photos and promotional tools, groom you and send you to clients when you are ready, and in the meantime, may also advance you funds and help you find lodging, if needed.

If the agency accepts you on a trial basis

They may put you on the testing board, if they have one, send you to hairdressers at your own expense, send you to photographers or give you a list of test photographers and have you make your own appointments. They will ask photographers for feedback on your potential.

An agency may advise you should not start in the market to which you have applied, but recommend you begin in a smaller one or recommend European experience, in which case they may become your mother agent and send you to their European counterpart.

Not now, maybe later:

Depending on the degree of the agency's interest, they may help you get your tests and composite through referrals to test photographers, and after you have put a good book together they may then want to sign you. Or you may be told to come back to see the agency at a later date, to reapply when conditions have changed – say during busy season, or when you have more experience, when you have made certain adjustments in your appearance such as weight loss, hair color, or consulted a dermatologist, orthodontist, plastic surgeon, etc.

Summer crash programs:

Some agencies oversee summer crash programs, and you may be invited to participate in one of these.

Fashion capitals accentuate development during summer months when school is out. At this time, an agency arranges housing, testing, and training, schedules visits to magazine editors who will look at a model's tests. The large agencies maintain apartments staffed by house mothers specifically for this purpose. Typically, the models who reside here are between 15 and 21. Or newcomers may share suites in midtown hotels. Some agencies maintain apartments both in New York and in a number of foreign cities, and a place may be found for you there as well.

Who pays initial expenses?

In 999 out of 1000 cases, you will be responsible to front all costs of a modeling career. In only a small percentage of cases will an agency be willing to foot the bills, which they usually do only if you are signed to an exclusive contract. Expenses will be recouped later, when you start earning.

It is possible that if you are sent abroad, the foreign agency may pay your expenses, if you are specifically requested by them. If you are sent to Japan, your Japanese agency will pay all expenses and will also guarantee you minimum earnings over a specific time period.

Alternatives

Determine what type of work you're suited for and what type of approach to take for the next step, if any. If you are wrong for one agency they may refer you to others. Some agencies will keep you on file and consult their files when specific types are called for – you may be contacted even a year or more later.

In New York, television commercial models work through several agents, so if your focus lies in this area, make sure you visit and are known to all the top commercial agents, who are union franchised. Lists of talent agents specializing in commercials and other jobs requiring more skills proliferate on the internet. Character people and older models, especially those with acting experience, will be wise to cast a wide net, making sure that everyone in a position to hire them is aware of their existence.

Remember also that it is always advisable to get a second opinion. Interview with several model agencies before settling on one you feel comfortable with. Of course, if you come from a small town, this is not always possible – if you hit the only game in town and they want you, by all means, go with them.

What you should know about a model agency:

Before you sign, you should feel confident that the agency is the right one for you, and sure that they are going to work for you. There are a number of things you will want to know to make certain you're in the right hands:

– Does the agency have affiliates in other cities and markets?

– How effective is this agency? Are they one of the top rung agents?

– Are they union franchised? (They should be).

– Do they represent many working models? What careers have they been responsible for? (On their walls, you may see faces you recognize. Ask about them).

– How big is the agency sales force? How many bookers do they have?

– How much money will you need to get started? Will they offer to advance you any funds?

What happens after you sign?

Don't expect immediate miracles. Usually, getting work will take time.

After you have signed with the agency or are on their testing board, it's time to start working on your look, polishing your image and abilities. Now you will be visiting photographers, getting test shots, taking classes, and working to improve your skills.

What to do if you're not accepted by a model agency

Do not despair and don't panic. Some of the most successful models were at first rejected by top agencies. If you really want to model, keep believing in yourself, but at the same time also reassess your assets and liabilities to see what you can do to change any negatives and accentuate strong points. Drawbacks are not insurmountable; strengths can always be highlighted to greater advantage. An initial setback may mean it takes longer to get going, but if you're determined, if you have the raw material to begin with, and if you persevere, you can conquer rejection.

Sometimes all it takes is upgrading your book. So experiment with different clothes, makeup, photographers, lighting, and concepts. Keep improving your image and presentation. Are you sure you're selling yourself in the best category? Are you the right height, weight and age for that category? If not, take stock, and try to fit into another area. Remember that modeling has room for many types.

Use everything in your environment as a learning tool. Visit libraries, museums, department stores, boutiques and fashion shows for inspiration and ideas. Be ever alert to anything that could spell a difference in your presentation.

Ask the agencies you interview with for advice and contacts. Try other markets if your first choice doesn't work out. Change your look if needs be, improve your skills through classes and study. Get a book together by yourself, go through all the steps this book outlines in testing, composites, headshots, and other model promotional tools. Start sending out your photo duplicates to agents, casting directors, ad agencies, and production houses yourself, and follow up with phone calls, requests for appointments and in person visits. Most casting people are receptive and will see you.

You might also find a personal manager and/or, budget permitting, a public relations person to help push your modeling career. You can find photographers listed in trade papers and online. Call on them for test shots, and try to learn the ropes on your own. This may be the only way to launch a career when the model is not a fashion type and no model or talent agency initially agrees to take him/her on without previous experience.

Aspiring show room models can find ads in Women's Wear and other industry publications, can visit merchandise marts to seek work on their own. In New York, such addresses as 550 7th Avenue and 1430 Broadway are good places to start looking for showroom modeling.

Sometimes the Sunday New York Times has ads for promotional models, as do newspapers in other cities. Word of mouth, talking to photographers and to other models you may meet can also help provide ins and information.

As a hopeful model without representation, you can visit performer union (SAG -AFTRA) bulletin boards for casting calls and open auditions; call advertising agencies and casting agents on your own, and pursue a career for a time without an agent. SAG-AFTRA sometimes offers classes and workshops, and can also steer you in the right direction for getting audio and video audition tapes of your work.

Above all, don't take rejection personally. Keep in mind that modeling is a competitive field, and not everyone you meet has time to nurture you. Their reasons for saying no can be as varied as a quirk in their personalities or as simple as getting up on the wrong side of the bed that morning. It's up to you to slough off negative reactions and keep going – just hit the next client on your list with an upbeat attitude. So maybe you'll get twenty, thirty rejections – or more. The trick is to keep refining your outlook, your personality and your presentation.

It takes time for a career to move into gear. Models are not made overnight, and the groundwork is always grueling and frequently discouraging. All models have described self-doubt from rejection suffered at the hands of decision-makers who rebuffed them and judged them harshly, but those models who persevered conquered failure and went on to success. Most people have no idea how much persistence it takes to become a model. If you really want this career, keep at it. You will learn, you will catch on, and sooner or later, your efforts will start paying off.

CHAPTER 2 -TRAINING, TESTING & MODEL SELLING TOOLS

Model Training

The agency may train you personally or send you out for training to their associates, such as hairdressers, makeup artists, and coaches. You may need classes, private lessons, or whatever the agency believes you require for grooming. You may receive an agency in-house makeover, or they may give you an agency booklet to read, study and apply.

When you are accepted by an agency, they will work hard for you, but you are expected to do your part. You will start testing and building your model's portfolio, the latter which will go with you everywhere. If an agency puts you on their testing board, the agency may either set up appointments for you, or tell you to refer to their list of photographers who do tests and set up your own photo appointments.

Even if you have not been accepted by an agency, you will still need test shots to start modeling, but you will definitely have to solicit photographers yourself and take the initiative to get those shots on your own.

If you have been accepted by an agency but they don't set up the appointments with test photographers, the agency may not have the time to fully devote to you, or they may want to get an idea of your how serious you are about modeling and how great is your ambition. Being a model is not only looking the part and being well groomed, it's taking the initiative, pushing and selling yourself. No model gets to the top by sitting back and waiting for the phone to ring. It's up to you to hit the streets, ring bells, knock on doors, ask people to look at you and test you, and not give up when they say no.

Test Shots

Testing enables you to get prints made either free or at a reasonable rate. Some photographers charge for tests, others do not; photographers today are not as willing as they once were to do free tests and some will ask you to split the film and processing costs.

Why do photographers test? A new photographer trying to get established may phone local agencies to request models for testing; a photographer or his assistant may be updating his portfolio and need a particular type or look. Photographers sometimes need test shots to try out new ideas, as do art directors who then assign work to photographers, who in turn, use models. Some catalog companies and stock houses shoot for stock; some photographers shoot on speculation, which might even lead to a job.

Some photographers do not want to test new models, others relish taking a blank canvas and making it into a great discovery.

What kind of pictures do you need to start working?

You will a variety of shots in both color and black and white – headshots, head and shoulders, full lengths, body shots, and 3/4 shots showing different angles, lighting, makeup, hairstyles, expressions, moods, and styles of photography, shot by several different photographers – studio shots, out of doors shots, photos using available (natural) light, and studio light.

Suggestions to keep in mind are: full length fashion shots showing legs; action shots, smiling shots, serious shots, sophisticated glamour shots, photos in which you wear exotic makeup and/or little to no makeup; profile pictures, a tight closeup for beauty and cosmetics; situational photos, such as mother and child, male and female model interacting, and product shots; at sporting and leisure activities; the model as homemaker, young mother, flight attendant, doctor, college kid, professional, bride, groom; attired in formal wear, sportswear, business wear, casual wear, exercise wear, swimwear, lingerie, and showing off accessories.

Eventually, your optimum photos will combine to create what is known as your portfolio or model's book. The best of these shots, in turn, will be duplicated for use on a composite, headshot or comp card to be sent to clients; and your agency will also use your best shots for their agency book, mini-portfolio and head sheet.

Sometimes the model and agency have a clear idea of what direction to go in on initial testings; other times, a model's look is developed over a long period of time.

Each photographer has his particular area of interest and expertise – high fashion editorial, catalog, beauty, glamour, a TV commercial look, an advertising look; some photographers deliver successful outdoorsy photos, others a contemporary man/business/office look. Likewise, models may be geared in one direction or another, better suited to one area than another. If you haven't determined your area of specialization, you may have to experiment to see what works best for you; or perhaps photographers will have a vision you can embody without realizing it.

When you're starting to test

Determine what type clients and work you are aiming for and what is needed to get them. Discuss what type photos you need with your agency and with each photographer. Spend time studying a photographer's work, identify what it is that appeals to you about it; think through what you want to accomplish with him, and ask him to try to shoot you in that manner.

Look through magazines and online for all types of photos – full length, close up, 3/4, studio, outdoors, etc., and use these as inspiration for your own photos.

What to ask a photographer before testing with him

Ask to see the photographer's book. Decide if his are the kind of shots you want. You will need to determine who is paying for the cost of film, processing, and contact sheets. What costs will be involved in the total package? How many prints for use in your book (and what size) will the photographer give for the quoted price? Can you buy extra prints, and if so, how much will they cost? Will the photographer retouch if needed, or can he recommend someone who will? Will you be given the negatives or will he retain them? (If the photographer retains the negatives, you will have to have copy negatives made if you want to use the photos to make glossies, composites, or comp cards).

Are these to be location or studio shots? Will the photographer provide a stylist, makeup artist and hairdresser, or will you be on your own? What clothes are you expected to bring, or will clothing be provided? Does the photographer have a wardrobe of stock items, including accessories and jewelry? How long before you can see a contact sheet or transparencies? Will the photographer refer you to others in the field who can forward your career?

What do you want in a photographer?

The modeling world is full of great photographers. How to find the ones that will suit your style? The best way is to interview them. You can find a list of test photographers in major market areas from Models Mart who will shoot either for free or for nominal sums.

When you are checking out a photographer's portfolio, ask yourself how current does it look? Does his work suit the image you want to project? Do you admire this photographer's work from a technical standpoint?

Photographers will often give suggestions on posing, clothes, product selection and use. Many photographers are of great help in teaching a model to free up, sometimes by offering advice, sometimes by establishing a rapport, even by playing music or telling funny stories, by complimenting the model, and mostly by transmitting subtle energies.

And by the way, if you're serious about a career in modeling, don't even consider using amateur photographers for your photographs. Work with the best professional photographers your city has to offer. Otherwise, you'll be wasting your time and doing yourself a disservice. The trained eyes who will be viewing your pictures can always spot the difference between a pro and a wannabe.

Remember

– If you are paying for the photos, get bids and estimates from several photographers.

– If the photographer's assistant or another fledgling photographer prints, your cost will be more reasonable..

– Know what you want to get and what you are getting. Make it clear what you expect, and that you will pay only on satisfaction.

Your first test shots

Bring several wardrobe changes to let the photographer choose what he thinks will be most effective. Sometimes the photographer won't want to photograph the items you bring and will offer alternatives from his own bag of tricks, but you should always show you are prepared and professional.

From your wardrobe, choose garments with attractive and varying necklines (turtleneck, cowl neck, crew, sweetheart, etc.) in flattering colors; bring jewelry that enhances your appearance, scarves and other eye-catching accessories. Bring a bathing suit and/or exercise wear, a leotard or tights, something that shows your figure to advantage. Select a business suit and casual wear or anything you think is appropriate to the type of modeling work you are aiming for. Often a simple blouse and skirt, or, for men, a casual shirt and chinos make a pronounced statement. Sophisticated formal wear is a good standard item, outerwear also a popular choice.

Capturing your image

You should orient your concepts toward anything that can highlight your image of young mother, housewife, nurse, girl next door, glamour girl, fashion, beauty or cover girl look; or in the case of men: young husband and father, business executive, hunk, nerd, sportsman, geek, etc. In some of your portfolio shots you will want to pose with products, either holding or using them, thus you might want to bring some with you on a test shoot – your iPad, a box of cereal, a well known brand of soap or shampoo, a bag of potato chips; or perhaps the photographer has usable items like these in his studio.

In some shots you might be pictured with a partner of the opposite sex or with an infant or child, in which case you should ask the photographer if he wants you to provide other models to pose along with you, or if he will provide them.

To determine what fashions and current outfits are best, check the European magazines, as European trends are ahead of ours. Use these ideas in your tests. Beauty shots should always contain current makeup and hairstyling. Anything that proves dated within six months should later be removed from your book.

If your personal wardrobe doesn't offer all you wish, borrow, rent or scavenge in a thrift shop. At the latter you might come up with treasures like wedding gowns, hats, eyeglasses, riding habits, attaché cases, towels, sweatbands, tennis racquets, exercise equipment, weights and other items that will make good additions to your test shot inventory.

Test shot check list

Consult magazines ahead of time to get ideas. Arrive early, with all basics done, hair ready to comb out, unless a stylist is being used, in which case you will come in clean and let them take over.

Over the course of the session, you must produce a continuous variety of expressions and moods. You should modify your hair with each outfit. If possible, vary the makeup; use different lipsticks, eye shadows, etc. Aim for naturalness and a lack of self-consciousness in front of the camera.

Test shot tips

The best tests come when specific ideas are executed, rather than guess work and shot-in-the-dark conceptualization. If you are doing outdoor shots, schedule early in the morning before noon, or later in the afternoon. Avoid outdoor shots in mid-day, which creates unflattering shadows.

All photographers see differently; no two are alike. Some shoot fast, some slow. Working with good photographers teaches a model. When the model is comfortable with the photographer and communication is good, something exciting comes through, and the tests are usually successful. Take your cues from the photographer; let him start things moving.

And be sure to get enough rest before the shoot.

When you see your proofs

Go over the shots. Examine the bad ones to see what you did wrong. The camera picks up details either unseen or seen differently by the naked eye, and as a model, you need to become aware of this.

Ask the photographer's opinion of your work, then take the proof sheet or transparencies to your agency to solicit their opinion.

Through review and discussion, determine which photos do the most for your marketability.

The photographer and your agency will let you look at the proofs through a loupe, so you can determine how your pictures will look when enlarged. Prints may have to be cropped, that is, cut off at a specific place during enlargement, for a better composition and effect.

To illustrate reactions to initial test shots, here are two brief passages from my bestselling novel **THE BEAUTY TRAP**. In the first selection, Eve, a teenage model just starting out, is looking at her first tests:

Eve was disappointed when she saw her first contact sheets. She looked awkward and tense. The poses seemed all wrong, and the photographer hadn't done a good job in the darkroom. She'd hoped for much better pictures, but the agency said not to worry.

"This is fine for a first group," Rex said. "Look, these two heads aren't bad at all. In fact, we can use them if he'll crop them right." He marked one of the pictures with a soft red pencil to illustrate what he meant, and Eve saw that he was right: minus the torso, which had been distorted, the picture was good.

"This is what test shots are for," Rex said. "It's always a pruning process. The pictures I've checked will be fine when they're blown up."

"Besides," Charlene said, "the photographer isn't one of the better ones around. I don't know why you picked him."

"She's seeing Franco next week," Rex said. "Then we'll really see some results."

In the next selection, Eve, helped by a great photographer, has improved:

Franco Gaetano had done some absolutely sensational photographs of Eve. To her surprise, he had made six blow-ups of his own choosing without even waiting for the agency to pick, and told her that if Rex and Charlene wanted others from the contacts, he'd make those too. Trembling with excitement, Eve almost ran to the agency.

"Let me see. I can hardly wait," Charlene said.

"Oh, baby, these are wild!" Rex exclaimed. "Fantastic, Eve!"

"This girl's going places. I knew it from the start. You've got enough of a book to begin working, Eve. Later you'll have twenty or more shots, but for now, this is fine to get you started."

"From here on," Rex said, "you're going to be working a lot; wait and see."

Enlargements for your book

Select photos that reproduce well – sharp focus, good contrast. The photographer himself may print, his assistant may, or you may have to take the negatives to an outside lab for printing. Your photos must always be top quality prints. If your photos need to be spotted or retouched, you may have to go outside to a custom lab or specialist for this, if the photographer does not include it in his service.

If photos need additional special attention, such as color correction, you will be told by the experts (the photographer and your agency). After a time you will spot the value in different photos yourself, but in the beginning listen to those who know, and do as they say.

You may be lucky to assemble a portfolio quickly, or it may take over a year to get just the right book that contains enough variety and enough appropriate shots. You may strike a wrong note at first, misjudge your type, or be wrongly perceived; you may need to work into a style that shows you to better advantage. Modeling is full of surprises – you never know when a moment will hit, when someone will just discover a side of you you never realized was there that makes all the difference in career direction.

Photo duplication

You are beginning to get your book together, which is an ongoing, ever-changing and never really completed process. But choices have to be made as soon as possible for reproduction, so clients can have your image and likeness in their files ASAP.

After print choices have been made, you will go to the next stage, duplicating your best shots, mass produced in large quantity. Multi-copying may take one of various formats:

– Headshot or glossy
– Comp card (also called "card," "Sed card," "Zed card" or "Z-card")
– Composite
– Post card
– All of the above
– Other

Regardless of which format you (and your agency) choose from the above list, you will need anywhere from a bare minimum of 50 up to a few thousand copies of your photos, at the agency's discretion (or at your own discretion if you have not signed with an agency). Each time you visit a client, you will leave one of your headshots (also called glossies), composites, comp cards, Sed cards, or other self-promotional tool that represents you to advantage.

Your agency can recommend where to go for multicopying; probably they have a specific place they always use. If not, and if you are wondering where to go, labs usually advertise in trade publications, as well online and in the yellow pages. A popular choice in New York City is Modernage, which has three convenient locations, but you may select from a wide variety of other labs as well. Ask these companies for samples, so you can judge the quality of their work.

Other matters to be decided for your photo duplicates include typeset, stock and print finish. Your agency can tell you if they want glossy, matte or semi-matte paper, card stock or paper stock. The agency may have a logo they want used. They may also recommend type face, or else you or the lab may decide. The model pays for printing costs except in unusual cases.

Your selling tools

Composites, headshots, comp cards, and post cards are chief among a model's promotional tools. Know what kind of work you are aiming for and select only your best shots to promote your look. Be sure that your photos represent you to advantage and that your pictures actually resemble you.

Composites and comp cards consist of a series of shots, anywhere from two to even up to ten or twelve, multi-copied on either a single page or on a more elaborate fold-out resembling a brochure, showing the model in a variety of moods, photographed with different lighting, clothing, angles, and positions, in headshot, full length, extreme closeup, and other varied photographic setups.

Both the composite and comp card should show range – sophisticate to young junior, for instance, businessman to nerdy father, etc. The conventional composite and comp card offer an animated, smiling headshot, body shot, product shot with full view of the hands, and possibly also a serious face as well.

For reproduction, you should always use top quality prints, in sharp focus.

Comp cards

Comp cards may vary in size. They may be one sided or two sided, six sided, printed on one side only or on two, using one or two photos or several, in color or black and white; they may also fold out, and may be printed on either card stock or paper stock.

The 5 x 8 inch comp card is also known as a Sed card , named for its inventor, Sebastian Sed, of the Parker-Sed Agency, Hamburg, Germany. It is also known as a "Zed" card.

Other popular sizes are 5 1/2 x 8 1/2, 6 x 8, 6 x 9; the card could be a double one, 5 1/2 x 17, folded in half, printed on four sides, using 4-10 photos, some of which might be reproductions of magazine covers.

The comp card should identify you by name and list your vital statistics -- height, weight, bust, waist, hips, shoe and dress sizes, hair and eye color, etc. If you are modeling in Europe you must also list European and British sizes, showing your measurements in metrics (centimeters and kilos instead of inches and pounds) and the British system (stones instead of pounds).

The comp card also shows where you can be reached, your home agency telephone and fax number, and the agencies you use abroad with their numbers. Some models list a half a dozen and more locations throughout the world.

Most fashion models use cards printed on 100 pound card stock.

Head shots, glossies

The head shot or glossy is generally used for commercials and acting jobs. A straight-on shot is preferred, looking right into the lens, showing a pleasant, animated expression, especially in the eyes. This headshot shows you as you are, not enhanced through special effects or a photographer's enhancement (although some retouching is permitted). Though you need not be exceptional looking, you must portray a unique look and represent the type character the client wants; your personality must emerge.

Glossies are 8 x 10 in size.

Resumes

Resumes are needed for all category of performers, for those who speak lines, do commercials and pursue acting jobs. The resume should be stapled to all four corners of the back of your glossy or composite. The resume should include your union affiliations, abilities, talents, credits, agency numbers and other pertinent information. List your special abilities; for example: "Dance: modern, jazz, tap, ballet; Sports: tennis, riding, sailing, golf; Music: piano and guitar;" list college degrees and advanced study, foreign languages, accents and impersonations. List your theatre, film, TV, and announcing credits, if any. For the beginning model/actor, credits may be little theatre, summer stock, or college productions rather than professional theater credits.

Resumes must be updated constantly. As soon as you have new credits, they go on your resume. You will either create the resume yourself and save it to disk, or if you're not adept at word processing, you will need to have the resume professionally done. Preferably, you will do the resume yourself, so that as you perform new work, it will be easier to add your updated credits.

Some models and actors omit TV commercial credits from their resume; it may be better to say "principal in over a dozen network commercials, list provided on demand," or something to this effect, so that a prospective client doesn't erroneously presume old credits are present conflicts. (A principal in commercials must be exclusive in that category; i.e., if the model is advertising Kellogg cereals, he may not also advertise Quaker Oats, and so on, until the commercial has run its course and is no longer being broadcast).

Composites

A composite consists of two or more photos on an 8 x 10 format, glossy; or the composite may be on paper stock, either 8 x 10, 8 1/2 x 11, or 8 1/2 x 17 folded in half, printed on four sides, or a fold out.

Your composite will list your age range, height, weight, experience, training, special skills, and so forth, as in the glossy, above.

Postcards

If you are doing something important you wish clients to be advised of, if you are appearing on a soap or have a special commercial airing at a particular time, for instance, you will want to have a post card printed up to send to your client list. Your photo will appear on one side, your message and the client's address on the other. You may purchase mailing labels, making the job easier.

Choosing a portfolio size

Your photo enlargements will go into a model's book, also called a portfolio. This book will accompany you everywhere you go, on all your rounds.

Portfolio sizes are available in several sizes. They come in sizes such as 9 by 12, 8 1/2 x 11, 8 x 10, 11 x 14, etc. Mini-portfolios are 5 x 7. The standard book for models is 9 x12 without zipper or handles, and is called a pressbook. The most popular portfolio today is the Scuba Book, so called because it is made of neoprene, the wet suit material and is extremely durable. This size is used mainly because it accommodates models' magazine tear sheets better than the 8x10 size portfolio. You will find portfolios of all sizes advertised online, so you can get an idea of the variety available, or an agency can direct you where to obtain one.

Portfolios should contain 10-24 or more reproductions, clippings and tear sheets, in protective non glare sheets, showing how you look in variety of situations, moods, angles, styles, in different outfits, makeup, and hairstyles. It's your agency's role to help determine the best shots for your portfolio. Keep your book with you at all times. Add to it, update it, and guard it with your life. It is your ticket to jobs and the most important key to your future in the modeling business.

Portfolio arrangement

A good portfolio is a model's most prized asset. As you continue in modeling, your book will change as you change, but it should always be an attention getter. Unless you organize the very best and most professional book, your presentation will not make the impression you are hoping for. Perfection is what you want in making a definite statement about yourself. And the statement you make on February 1st is not the same statement you will make on August 1st. Modeling is fluid, evolving, changing, and dynamic. A good eye will recognize anything dated or derivative. If it's last season, it may not work this season.

The photos in your book, protected behind acetate sleeves, reflect your talents. Depending on your type, you will want to emphasize different moods and looks: teen shots, preppy, collegiate, sophisticate, young mother, businesswoman, etc., showing a different face for each, a winning smile, radiant skin, various qualities – perhaps wit, humor, or quirkiness, each shot attesting to what categories and to what extent you can fill the bill for whatever is called for.

Depending on the type of work you are best suited for, or whether you are looking to fill more than one category, you will want a versatile portfolio that speaks well for your experience, how you work with different photographers, and your ability to sell products, be they clothes, cosmetics, cell phones, cereal, computers, or whatever. Your book will contain good head shots, the best of your full lengths, tear sheets from magazines, shots from fashion shows – sportswear, furs, and swim wear from a junior look to haute couture; you may be photographed on an exercise machine or in an action shot, clad in athletic wear; young business-attired executive on the move, body shots, location and product related shots, happy, serious, sensual, "attitude" shots – the possibilities are endless, as creative as you and your varied photographers can be.

Photo order

It is best to open your book with a good strong head shot, followed by two fashion shots. A body shot might come next, then casual shots, outdoorsy, beauty, and more heads to break things up. Both color and black and white can be utilized to advantage, in a cumulative effect that creates a definite pace and rhythm. Arrange your shots so that the book ends with a bang, for final impact.

It's a good idea to have your best shot first, the second best shot last. Strongest shots should be placed on the right hand side of the book, as the eye travels there first. Be aware of varying clothes, backgrounds, props, accessories, and dramatic situations. Don't let anything overpower or distract in pictures facing each other. Keep away from duplicates or near duplicates; never repeat anything similar twice.

Though eventually you will be aiming for 24 good pictures, 10 is all right in the beginning, and at the very outset, even four great ones may do to get your foot in the door. You have to build from somewhere; your book puts you on the market, announces you are a professional model for hire, and propels you toward work.

As you move ahead in your career, your book will change as you meet new clients and land new assignments. Keeping your book current is a constant process of blending new shots and tear sheets with older ones. You are always trying to supplement, augment, round out and update. Keep on testing. Your book should be in continuous flux. Never be satisfied with it. Renew it on a constant basis.

If you don't keep updating, some clients whom you visit time after time may get tired of seeing the same book and will comment that your book isn't current, or ask you point blank, "How current is your book?" Never lie about it (all the more reason to keep updating).

If at first you can't discern between photos that work and those that don't, get advice from those in the know – agents and photographers, casting people, and other professionals. In time, you too will come to know this like second nature. Changes happen, and your look may become obsolete unless you are quick to reinvent yourself. Whether consciously or unconsciously, a model is always assimilating. The successful model, male or female, enjoys the benefit of meeting people at the top of their profession – photographers, advertising agency executives, designers, editors, and fashion experts, contact with whom helps the model aware of keeping the look updated.

CHAPTER 3 - ROUNDS , SEEING CLIENTS & MARKETING YOURSELF

Initial promotion

Once you have picked up your hundred, two thousand or whatever quantity of photo duplicates ordered, you are ready to begin modeling rounds in earnest. Rounds are what a model does in calling upon potential clients. Modeling is a continual search for new clients, which necessitates constant rounds, at the very least until the model has built up a reliable client list, and even then some.

Especially at the outset of your career, you have to make people aware of who you are. This is done by both the model and the agency distributing photos, by the model going out on appointments, auditions, interviews, go sees, etc., and by the agency sending the model's portfolio or mini-portfolio out to be inspected by photographers, advertising agencies, magazines, production houses, casting directors, and others in a position to hire. It's advisable to supplement your agency's efforts with efforts on your own;

A model gets assignments through contacts already nurtured so that those clients rebook, as well as through new clients acquired through picture submissions, followed by go sees and interviews, all of which comprise part of the model's rounds. Look sees, calling on photographers, audition callbacks and cattle calls are also loosely categorized under rounds.

How long will it take to get work?

There are no set rules. The development stage ends when your portfolio is ready to be seen. If you are extraordinarily lucky, you might work instantaneously, but don't count on it.

More than likely, it will take you a few months or more, possibly even more than a year to get going. It depends on circumstances and the model, market climate, your pictures, the clients you meet, work availability and a numerous other factors, including being at the right place at the right time. One thing is certain: tastes will change, and it won't take long for your pictures to be outdated. Hence, the constant need to modify your book.

Look-sees and other stops

As you make rounds, show your book, drop off composites, and get to know clients, you will come to know how intense competition is in the modeling field, and how much constant push and steady discipline is required in the profession.

For many models, it's not easy to make his/her own calls, but sometimes it's the only way. Often a model is in the position of having to do a great deal of the pushing himself. Lauren Hutton, one of the most successful models of all time, tells how she was rejected by all the top agencies in the business, until finally being accepted by one. To start the ball rolling, Lauren's agency would arrange four appointments a day for her, and she would set up six more herself. From all this, perhaps one or two little jobs would result over a several week period. To supplement her initially small income, Lauren worked as a fit model. In modeling, it can take a long time for the steam to build, but if you keep the faith, your efforts can pay off, as Lauren Hutton testifies.

It's a good idea to set a quota for seeing a certain number of clients per week. Even though the marketplace has a consistent appetite for new faces, you must seek out clients aggressively. Even when you start getting jobs, you have to continually make efforts, push and upgrade yourself. It could take months to get your footing, longer to become established, and even longer yet to make it on a loftier level.

So consult your client list and make it a point to accomplish a set number of calls every day. Make appointments for geographical convenience, scheduling them in the same location so that you don't have to be dashing back and forth between distant locations. Contact photographers area by area, starting downtown; then start over and go through the list again. Be sure to check in frequently with your agency.

As you make rounds, continue testing. Study magazines, films, TV, catalogs, fashion pictures in newspapers for new ideas.

Reasons to see a client

When you visit a potential client as part of your rounds, you should always have a definite, stated reason for being there. State this purpose to the person who greets you.

What are some of the reasons to see a client? Newly arrived models never before seen by a client are always welcome, since new faces are constantly sought; If you have something new to show – new composite, new tear sheets; if you have just returned from out of town, especially from European experience; if you have added new content to your book; you mailed something – such as composite, comp card or tear sheet to the client, and would like a personal meeting, face to face; you have new credits that have been added to your experience; you have created a new look, you have done something new and exciting; you have just changed agencies; you have an audition or booking in the same area and wanted to drop by; or you are interested in testing with them. You may think of other reasons, but these are a start.

What they want and why they want it:

Clients will be asking themselves when they meet you and look through your book, what is special about this model? In some cases the answer is hard to pinpoint, just as beauty is in the eyes of the beholder.

What is a client looking for, and how does a model fit the image?

Sometimes the client doesn't even know what he wants, but wants to be surprised. In general, however, the model is judged by his book, his personality, and how he relates to the client and the product, how he could represent the product and suit the image the client needs to sell.

A client may pick a particular model that no one else liked, but the client is the one with the final say – he knows what he wants, what works for him, and what appeals to him is what is chosen.

Sometimes a model's arresting quality is in large measure an attitude, even one set up by the photographer or the editor, with the model's resulting success being an ego trip for them. In the case of fashion, it might be a style or a mood. It could be the way the clothes look on the model, something about the way that model comes alive in a particular lighting, or perhaps it's an ineffable touch, a certain movement, a head cocked a special way, attention drawn to a particular feature, a bowed head or an arrogant one, a long neck, and so on. It could be what in Milan is called a sguardo – a look that goes beyond a look, a look that is becomes a strong, meaningful quality; or what the French refer to as chien, as in elle a du chien, (chien literally means "dog," but obviously is untranslatable as such in English).

In too many cases, the client will think a model is just fine, there's nothing wrong with her, but ... and for some inexplicable reason, the model won't get the job. The fact is, there are so many great models out there in every world market. From a group of incredible models all with fabulous books, it is sometimes hard to say what will be the factor that makes one particular model stand out in the crowd. Personality, yes; yet sometimes even that is not the deciding factor. On the one hand, the marketplace constantly demands new faces, yet paradoxically, it takes time to break in. Seldom does success happen overnight. For the industry to recognize you means a couple of years, usually, and maybe even longer.

Is any new model that indispensable? No. Not till proven, and sometimes not then, either. A series of pretty pictures in Vogue,

Elle, Marie-Claire, Harper's Bazaar, a nicely photographed catalog session, even a high profile national commercial, are not in themselves enough. It takes a steady stream of ongoing assignments to become recognized and respected as a pro. In modeling, you really do have to pay your dues, just as in any other profession.

Go-See Protocol

Getting bookings can require several callbacks; little can be accomplished on a first interview, especially if it's just a general go-see with no definite purpose. What you can do in this case, however, is try to leave a lasting impression. Look people in the eye as you greet them, and offer your hello with a friendly smile. First impressions are important – you have all of about 30 seconds to get their attention, and another few minutes to reinforce it. Be personable yet businesslike. Answer all questions honestly and openly, be polite and unassuming when accepting compliments.

Be sure to have an ample supply of composites, comp cards, glossy heads or whatever is needed, to leave with the client. Someone in the studio may also take a Polaroid for identification purposes. You may be asked about availability and conflicts, whether you are adept at doing your own hair and can vary the style. Chances are unlikely you will be told on the spot if you have the assignment; in most cases, your agency will be the bearer of these tidings. The client will probably say, "We'll get back to you -- we'll be in touch with your agency."

You must never look desperate, fearful, angry or unhappy – all put offs. You are always on, always sparkling no matter how tired or down you feel. Each new client and each new go-see require adapting; in every case, you have to embody the client's look, and convince him you're exactly what he's looking for.

Marketing strategies

Any time you have anything noteworthy going on, a fashion spread, a record album cover, a commercial, a bit in a film or play, TV soap, even a walk on – promote it. Send out notices and post cards to all in sundry, post something on your website and/or your blog. Use social media – Facebook, Twitter, Google Plus, Tumblr, Flicker, etc. Post YouTube videos of yourself. These make good conversation pieces, especially when you are seeing the same people again. (In the modeling business, you will always see most of the same people over and over again).

Mailing lists on self-stick labels are advertised online (Models Mart and other websites) and in the trade papers. Xerox or scan these for repeat future use, save them on your hard drive to be printed out on Avery labels for reuse the next time around. Post on Facebook and Twitter.

Reel and Voice Tapes

Once you have film and/or video clips, you can make up a reel. A video of your commercials, clips, acting scenes or assignments demonstrating your skills can be distributed to casting and talent agents, ad agencies, production companies, and others.

Many model agencies have video facilities allowing the model to view himself on camera, in order to see how he comes across and determine what needs to be done to improve. Video yourself there or anywhere else you can.

If you want voiceover jobs, announcing or jingle work, you will need a studio-produced tape/cassette. Studios advertise their services online and in trade papers. You may also locate them through your agency or through the performers' unions. A voice tape should contain a sampling of your different type voices, spoken or singing. Have a hundred or more copies made and send out to agents and clients. The tape may contain your photo or logo on the front for additional self-advertising.

Often, online job sites will request videos of a model for specific jobs that are casting. Be sure you have something ready to be viewed when this happens.

Agency head sheets and mini-portfolios

Most agencies make up a head sheet of all its models, which it sends out to clients. These head sheets are updated on a regular basis, As a member of the agency roster, you will appear on its sheet and clients may request you to come in for a look see.

If a model makes up a mini-portfolio, she will give a copy to the agency to send out for clients' closer inspection. Mini-portfolios may closely approximate the photos in the model's own personal portfolio. The mini-portfolio will be sent out for a client's inspection when the model is unavailable for a go-see, and will be sent back to the agency. Many agencies keep on tap a few mini-portfolios of busy models who travel frequently or are always booked.

Other agency promo tools

In its constant seeking to promote you, the agency will need to have a large number of your composites, comp cards, and head shots on tap, to be sent out as job calls come in. You will also be in the agency's promotional book that displays one or several photos of each of its models, also sent out to clients. (The promotional book may be as small as 5 x 7 or as large as 11 x 14). Agencies also have bigger presentation books in 16 x 20 format which can accommodate larger size magazine spreads and photos of their models' work world wide.

All of the above are used in agency preliminary selling the model to clients. Additionally, some agencies may schedule parties and fashion shows, luncheons, cocktail gatherings, and other special events, so clients and models can meet one another.

Always keep in mind

You are a commodity, desired for your image and for your ability to project that image, to the degree that it is right for the product or service you are selling. Compare yourself to other models. Ask what sets you apart from others in your age range and type? What clothing is best for you? What colors, what styles become you? How can you be seen to optimum advantage? How can you best showcase your physical appeal?

Look through magazines to get ideas. Consult agents and photographers as well as the stylists, hairdressers and makeup artists you work with. Everyone will have a different opinion, but you can start learning to be objective.

No model makes it on looks (or "look") alone. A model has to project personality no matter where. A model's flair and individuality must stand out; a model must have impact and must draw attention to the product or service he is selling.

Social skills, facility in interacting with people are important. Be cheerful and cooperative no matter what the situation. Modeling is a small world in which word travels fast. If you are temperamental or hard to work with the modeling world will surely hear about it. Nobody makes it alone; you need people behind you to help you reach the top. So be appreciative, thank others for their help; be enthusiastic, outgoing, on time and prepared; give your best; and always be friendly toward others in the business.

Dressing for modeling: clothing and accessories - your wardrobe

A model needs a basic business wardrobe for go-sees as well as a professional wardrobe to use when the job requires personal wardrobe. Sometimes wardrobe will be provided by the designer or other client, but many times the model must bring his or her own clothing, which usually means several selections for the client to choose from.

Wardrobe for auditions, go sees, and other interviews:

Dress in a way that reflects your type and personality, enhances your look and image. Whenever you have been given information about the job, dress for the client. Some models are extremely casual in their attire, wearing jeans, baggy boyfriend jackets, men's shirts, and stretch tops. If you know the client and have worked for them before, this might be acceptable attire to arrive for a job where you're going to pose in the client's choice of wardrobe, but you should dress up for important go sees, particularly if you are a newcomer or if you are meeting non-industry people such as a businessman client who is not too familiar with models. The beginning model needs to be more formal than the veteran. Leggings and neat, tailored trousers are all right, but initially, no jeans, please – although jeans are okay for established models.

On general go sees, your attire should be compatible with the photos in your portfolio. Play up your best features; highlight your strong points. Choose basic, comfortable, simple clothing that fits well and shows your body to advantage. Suits and figure flattering outfits are best.

Many models find soft pastels and neutral colors adapt well as wardrobe basics; navy, black, white, grey, and beige are good basics that can be accessorized creatively, and are versatile enough for most modeling purposes, excellent for go see wardrobe pieces, especially when you want to leave things to a client's imagination. However, for tests and jobs calling for the model's personal wardrobe, cameramen and photographers sometimes prefer to use something more colorful.

Study how colors can enhance your look. Sometimes a vivid hue will be just the thing that sets you apart from the pack. If you have a unique, individual style or trademark and come to an interview looking different and unusual and if you carry it off, editors and photographers may just love it. Conservative clients, however, could be turned off. Try to find out ahead of time what type client you are meeting and gear your look to his preferences and the sort of job you are going after. Your agency will help you decide.

When applicable, know the season, style and color appropriate for each specific go see. Does the interview call for your looking wholesome and All American, casual, teen, young mother, business executive? Does your choice of wardrobe suit the corporate image? Some clients, such as Procter and Gamble, are very conservative and would not care to see a blatant sexual play with attention-getting cleavage, whereas other clients would find it exactly the thing they've been waiting for.

You should also take into consideration proportion, the length of skirt, leg appearance, your comfort level, and the shoes you're wearing.

Building a basic modeling wardrobe

Some garments are more flattering than others. You should always be on the lookout for clothing that will enhance your appearance. Collect pages from magazines of the styles you like and think would look well on you. When you find a spare minute in your busy day, stop in and browse in department stores and boutiques; when possible, try on garments to check how they look on you. As a model you should become aware of fabrics, the feel and texture of silk, cotton, wool, linen; colors, designs and patterns.

European women, particularly French women, are known for their fashion sense and their talent for accessorizing. Study European fashion magazines or flip through them on the newsstand. Notice upcoming trends. Note hair, makeup, and accessories being featured in Europe. Also, become a regular reader of American fashion magazines and of such fashion industry publications as W and Women's Wear.

Undergarments

Women will need a wardrobe of foundation garments. Nude colored undergarments are best. You want at least one strapless bra as well as other types of bras with adjusting straps that accommodate halter tops, backless dresses, and other special necklines. One popular bra style on the market has convertible straps that can be used for five different necklines. Bust pads, body suits, a basic flesh colored body stocking, and half slips (one in taffeta to resist static) are basic items you should keep for professional use. Black undergarments are also de rigueur.

Personal wardrobe for assignments

For assignments in which you are expected to provide your own wardrobe, you should be prepared with an array of choices. Make sure you own a neutral toned suit, two or three skirts in neutral colors and pants in all season fabrics; a dark suit and slacks; jeans; silk and cotton blouses and shirts and t-shirts; knit, shell and tube tops; sweaters, two or three basic dresses, a business suit, and evening wear. Your wardrobe should reflect a variety of different necklines – jewel, square, ballerina, plunging, halter, décolleté, and so forth.

Shoes

For daily trudging from appointment to appointment, you have to be comfortable yet look good at the same time. You may need to carry an extra pair of shoes around with you in your model's tote. A basic shoe wardrobe requires several pairs, including pumps, flats, and dressy shoes; loafers, clogs, boots, summer shoes, sneakers, and sandals.

What to wear on a busy day when you have several go sees

If you have several interviews scheduled in one day, and need to assume different looks, it might be a good idea to wear something basic, then add or remove an item from your attire, assuming your go sees are for different purposes. In that case, try to strike a happy medium by choosing something that can be made more versatile by being dressed up or dressed down, using accessories like necklaces, scarves, belts, a sweater or a jacket.

The male model wardrobe

For testing, commercials and advertising print, a male model frequently is asked to provide his own wardrobe and shoes. Men should have an adequate supply of different blazers, casual wear and suits. They need a variety of ties in different colors and designs; dress clothes, casual clothes, shorts, bathing trunks; at least two business suits in tropical blend, winter blend, and all season. Brooks Brothers type sports jackets and blazers are necessary, as is a tuxedo, jeans, and business and sports shirts.

For tests, men need a versatile wardrobe suited to the type they are portraying: they will be photographed variously as the all American guy, young dad with a kid on his knee, at a restaurant having a romantic candle lit dinner with his wife; canoeing or hiking in the out of doors; smoking a cigarette or cigar; dressed in jeans, work boots, and a flannel shirt; wearing a sports glove or carrying a tennis racquet; smiling in a tux with hands in pockets, attired in a business suit in an office situation; in bathing trunks carrying a surfboard;, long pants rolled up; seated in an airline or at a computer; at a resort playing golf or horseback riding. Relating to a child is good; enacting a doctor, short order cook, waiter, truck driver, cop, construction worker, businessman or family man are other possibilities.

Responses and feedback

All potential jobs are different – sometimes the client is interviewing very few people, other times it's a cattle call. Everyone will have a separate opinion, and everyone will treat you differently. Some people will prolong an appointment and keep you late, making you rush to your next go see, while others will dismiss you in a few seconds – not that either method is any yardstick of how well you did on the interview; sometimes when you least expect you'll get the job, and when you're sure you've got it you find you were all wrong for it, that the client has something totally different than you in mind.

Maybe they are definitely interested; maybe they have no interest at all, or maybe it's a no this time, but they'll want you for something in the future. It can be hard to read what the response is; it could be the reverse of what you think – they loved you, they hated you, and you thought it was just the opposite.

As a model, however, you should always try to get feedback – ask your booker, your agency, and work on the feedback. What kind of impression did you make? If something constructive was said, pro or con, you may have something worth considering. If a client criticized your makeup, said your hair was a bad color, said something pertinent about your book, ask yourself whether they have a point or not.

Sometimes, you must disregard criticism and stick to your guns. Other times, you'll get no feedback at all. Or you may not get an immediate job offer but end up with compliments and an affirmation that you're doing things right.

Slow seasons

Always plan ahead. Know which seasons you can look forward to being busy in and which are the slow times, when your career will surge or plunge in activity. These may vary according to the city you are working in; however, it is possible to keep busy year round if you work in several markets.

Early fall and spring are collection months for buyers, followed by retail fashion shows, which are held closer to the actual season. Christmas promotions are photographed four to six months in advance, during summer. Holiday time, December and January, as well as summer vacation time are usually slow. During these periods, you can do productive things like adding tests and working on your next composite. Seize the opportunity to get seasonal shots, beaches, swimming, snow, ski and skating backgrounds, and other outdoor photos. If you are an actor as well as model, you may want to do summer stock to add to your credits and round out your experience.

Dealing with rejection - again and again

Just as you may have had to face rejection at the initial stage from an agency, you will experience many such repeats from clients. Get used to it.

You'd be surprised how many well known models, including some of the best known names in the business, have been told no, sorry, we can't use you, you're all wrong – and far worse. Down the line, all top models have experienced rejection and sometimes even humiliation. It takes not only perseverance to make it as a model, but a strong ego and a thick skin. You have to believe in yourself in spite of adverse comments and sometimes downright rudeness.

Knowing how to take rejection, putting it in perspective, understanding where it's coming from (a jealous editor? resentful account executive? rejected photographer?), based on what criteria (are you definitely wrong for the job? is your hair really the wrong color? are you the wrong age and size?) and how to discern the helpful from the destructive are all important parts of a model's awareness of handling a career.

If you receive adverse criticism, ask yourself if the criticism can be turned into something constructive that will help you improve yourself,

Tips to help advance your career

Be well groomed, professional, receptive to suggestions. Always dress the part. If you are called to be a career /businesswoman/executive, dress appropriately: wear a conservative suit, comfortable heels, a simple hairstyle, and subtle makeup. Don't show up in worn looking jeans with an armload of tattoos.

Keep your book current. Update constantly. Make calls to see what's going on, especially when you have not seen some people in a while or have been out of town. Send updates on your activities – tear sheets, post cards, greeting cards. You can scan photos of your tear sheets into your computer and send them electronically, as long as you have the client's email address (with his approval for use). Your agent will guide you to clients, but at the same time you can't sit back and wait for things to happen – you have to go out and make them happen.

Invest money, time, and energy in your future. Leave nothing to chance; do your utmost to leave no stone unturned. Your product is yourself, so you have to be your own best advertisement. As a marketable commodity, your presentation is crucial. Attitude, projection, personality, performance, self assurance and self esteem are all vital to your success. You must rise above personal problems, and be a complete pro on all interviews and assignments.

CHAPTER 4 - MODEL CATEGORIES & CASTING BREAKDOWNS

What type assignments are you right for?

Models are hired to work in print assignments, television commercials, wholesale/ retail /runway, designer and manufacturer showrooms, and live demonstrations.

In print modeling, a model may work in four categories: Editorial, Advertising, Catalog, and Publicity.

Editorial print

Editorial work is created by magazine and newspaper editors, rather than by paying advertisers. Editorial print highlights new trends, looks and ideas and is often shot on location. Models in editorial fashion are chosen for their style and uniqueness, or because they accurately reflect the concept an editor or photographer is striving for.

A model seen in prestige editorial assignments becomes instantly in demand – catalogs, designers and manufacturers will all want to use her. Many models parlay editorial exposure into other areas – TV commercials, beauty endorsements, runway work, and additional channels that can lead to greater and greater exposure.

Only a few magazines impact on a career. Among the best tear sheets are from bi-annual Sunday fashion supplements in *The New York Times*, and in the American and European editions of major fashion publications. However, a total of only about 100 prestige fashion pages per month exist in the USA, and only about 15 models get all the work. For this reason, most fashion models have international careers spanning several countries. Covers provide great editorial exposure, with important jobs making the difference between a good career and a fabulous one. Freshness and innovation, originality, and spontaneity in a model are qualities prized by fashion editors. Editorial wages are the lowest in modeling, but its cachet makes up for it.

Fashion editors are deluged with candidates and rarely will choose a total novice for their layouts, although sometimes fashion models completely new to modeling may just strike a chord with the powers that be, who then do decide to hire her. Realizing that such and such a photographer works well with novices, the editor might hire the new face on an impulse, and be pleased to have discovered someone who will be talked about in the industry. Finding new models can be an ego trip for both editor and photographer.

There is a constant flow of models on a daily basis, showing up with their portfolios at fashion magazines such as Vogue, Elle, Marie-Claire, Harper's Bazaar, and others. The model is first sent to the editor, then dispatched to various editorial departments – fashion, beauty, accessories, shoes. After this, she could be sent over to a photographer who is shooting a special assignment, if the staff decides she's right for it. The decision of what model to use is the last one to be made; first decisions involving clothing selection and layout.

Bookings can sometimes happen on a whim, perhaps based on a joint inspiration the editor and photographer experience about the model. However, the editor is central in fashion, and it is she who has the final decision. Even so, editorial fashion could not exist without collaboration between editor, stylist, photographer, and model.

Overexposure can happen. If a model is seen too much, particularly seen in a rival publication (unless she's a celebrity model or film star), fashion editors will stop using her. To spread the risk, a model looks to expand horizons abroad in a market like Milan, Paris, London, orTokyo. Of course, New York editorial work creates demand in the Euro markets.

Publicity regarding fashion models has increased enormously over past decades. Today the public recognizes fashion models as stars, whereas formerly only people in the industry knew them. While in the past models were seldom if ever identified by name, today one sees models identified in captions and on magazine covers. Increasingly, editorial work has become publicity for the designer and sometimes for the model as well, whether the model is mentioned by name or not. Both designers and models are now celebrities in their own right.

The bulk of high fashion work is usually done in the beginning of a model's career. Once she is established, seen in fashion pages for a certain length of time and has had exposure in other mediums, the editor will look elsewhere for talent. You have to strike a median for exposure and overexposure. Though overexposure inevitably does happen, hopefully by then the model will be at a new level in other directions, making more money than she would from editorial work.

Catalog Modeling

Catalog print work is steady and reliable, once the model is established. All ages and a broad range of photographic types are used. Catalog is demanding, requiring many setups featuring different garments shot during the course of a day. Catalog models must not only deliver a thoroughly professional performance, but must also often do their own hair and makeup. Each shot requires a change of pose and each new setup requires a different hairstyle.

Particular garment features must be emphasized. Models must know how to show off the clothes, highlight their best qualities and compensate for flaws, keep garments from bunching up, and so on. You must draw attention to the clothing's strong points, accommodate angles that work best, display to advantage a garment's details (like pockets, sleeves, buttons). You must sell the garment you are wearing in a way that your appearance never overshadows or detracts from the clothing.

Since catalog shoots deal in volume, the photographer can't spend a lot of time on each shot, therefore the model has to be able to handle setups quickly and professionally. The ability to pose, to move into new positions automatically and keep the expressions alive are important in catalog work.

Catalog print offers one of the best modeling opportunities for immediate dollars. It is a fast paced, no nonsense, very businesslike atmosphere in which there is no time for excuses, lapses, inability, or horsing around. Editorial often comes with a relaxed attitude and has room for pranks and jokes, but catalog, the "bread and butter" of modeling, definitely does not.

Catalog volume is huge, with the US market leading the way, and Germany and Japan also representing large markets as well. A model who lands a prime catalog account can be kept constantly busy and earn great money. In addition to the well known catalogs, there are countless small regional stores and specialty books, many of which are photographed in the secondary markets. The New York Public Library contains a list of over 50,000 US catalog enterprises that hire models.

If catalog work is prolific, it also comes with some of the most rigid rules and requirements. It is not only demanding but can be grueling. The model must keep up the energy level no matter how tired she may be. Every frame must be different, each emphasizing important features of a garment, perhaps the shortness of a jacket or the line of a skirt. It is up to you, the model, to know how to do all this quickly and without hesitation.

Catalog lighting is not always easy to work under, since it is apt to be harsh. Sometimes the model is uncomfortable, not only because of the lights but because of being literally sewn into, pinned or clothes-pinned into a garment. Sometimes the model can't turn because of a stain on the sleeve that must be kept out of sight.

There is no retouching in catalog work. Photographers allow only 15 to 20 minutes per shot, so time is of the essence. A catalog model must deliver or he/she will not be rebooked.

Catalog model selection

Catalog work is usually assigned through a joint decision of client, art director, photographer and stylist agreeing on whom to book. Unlike editorial print work, catalog uses no editors. In catalog, the fashion coordinator replaces the editor, but does lacks the autonomy of a top editor.

If you are called on a catalog go see, the first time will usually be for just look see, to show your book, and the second time to see the client. Catalog models must be well groomed and attractive, but not so stunning that they take attention away from the apparel. Height requirements for catalog models are roughly the same as for models in editorial fashion. The same catalog models are used 95% of the time.

Catalog booking lengths

A catalog model is usually booked half days, longer if necessary. Successful catalog models can be kept busy for days, weeks, months on end. A newcomer might get a short one or two hour booking as a trial, work half a day the next time, which could be as far as a couple of months down the road or possibly sooner. Often, a model gets the initial shot at catalog work due to another model canceling. Some agencies have a four hour minimum requirement, particularly for established models.

How much money can a catalog model make?

Roughly in the area of $10,000 - $15,000 for five days' work in top markets is possible, depending on the model's popularity and agency negotiation. Lesser known models will command less. Some models in secondary markets earn $125-$250 an hour or $850-$2500 per day. Children's rates are less than adults'.

What is expected in a catalog shoot?

Since very seldom in catalog is there a makeup man or hairdresser, you must do your own hair and makeup and be able to change and vary your look from shot to shot.

You should arrive with hair and makeup already done, prepared to model 20 different outfits in different setups, using the same lighting for single, double, and group shots, full lengths and 3/4 shots (the majority are 3/4 cropped). You are expected to know how to do make up for catalog work, allowing your makeup to compensate for any facial problems you have, such as too full a face, hollows, deep-set eyes, etc. The model should adjust makeup for strobe, filters, and other technical considerations. How the clothes look is of single concern, and there is no room for going over budget – you must deliver or you not only won't be rebooked, but your lack of professionalism will be a blight on your reputation.

Catalog work is almost always shot in studio settings. The photographer will tell the model if a shot is vertical, horizontal, or square. Catalog is quick, hard work, done through typecasting. Attitudes are important. The model's image must speak to a public who will be buying from that particular catalog.

The model must convey the right message by assuming different positions, expressions, and movements, showing a steady, ready range of poses in short order – fold your arms, place a hand on a hip, swing a limb, move in the opposite direction from the hemline, bend a knee, always with emphasis on the clothes. You must keep moving during the shoot, to make each frame different.

A model's movements for catalog work are usually simple and minimal, though sometimes, a pose will have to be held for long periods of time without moving. To vary a pose, a model varies technique, sometimes alternating weight on one foot and then the other; other times moving or walking in place, changing direction, shifting arms and hands, tilting the head, pausing, repeating, then beginning again, each time with minor variations. Often a rhythm is established between the photographer and model; sometimes this rhythm is also affected by the use of strobe, which is recharged after each use.

Catalog tricks

Never show the inside of a shoe or the inner thigh. A handbag is always held with its clasp on the outside, the way it opens. Never show the label on a scarf. A model is expected to know these things. In fashion editorial work, beginners can be reminded of pointers – there is more indulgence for not knowing; but in catalog, there just isn't time to deal with someone who doesn't know the ground rules.

Advertising print

Clients pay thousands of dollars to advertise their products in print media, in magazines and newspapers, on product packages, posters and billboards. All types of models are used in these ads, from children to fashion models, men of all types, real people and character types.

Advertising pays well; payment, in addition to the initial booking fee, may involve bonuses and buyouts; contracts may have escalations governing how and where a model's image is used, called usage fees, in which additional fees are collected for each individual photo and likeness usage, such as billboard, packaging, and other extended usage. If the photo will be seen in another part of the world, that too constitutes usage.

Any usage changes must be renegotiated. The agency always wants to know: where will the ad run? Worldwide? South Africa? South America? China? In all cases, varying usages are carefully pinpointed; there are usage options past initial periods, with many complex clauses to be renegotiated.

Large national advertisers may want to use a model exclusively based on one year or have an option for additional years. Products such as hair coloring in which hair is retouched many different times for various different colors pay usage fees for each separate color. It is not unusual for models who travel and work internationally to find their image and likeness plastered on billboards, packages and magazines the world over – in Japan, Brazil, Eastern Europe, and everywhere; in each separate case, a usage fee has been negotiated.

Holding periods of two months, six months, a year and even longer can be negotiated, in which in exchange for a certain fee, a model may not work for a rival company during a set period of time. A holding period can hinder a model if the competitor is willing to pay more for her services during this time frame, but often this is not known ahead of time and amounts to the breaks of the game.

Agencies are cautious that clients not tie up a model without appropriate compensation, and a model should always pay attention to what he/she is asked to sign. When placing your signature on a release, you should make sure that "usage" is only that which was agreed to by your agency. In a release asking for additional usage, the model can cross out anything he/she is unsure of, or may add agreed upon picture and usage information to a voucher, and initial the changes before signing.

Every print ad not only has a precise point of view, but aims for a specific audience. Cosmetics advertising is mostly done for image; image advertising in beauty is largely to get the product name in front of the public; in fact, 25% of a cosmetic company's total budget is used to establish image.

A company researches to decide to what model they will give an exclusive endorsement contract. The percentage of people who recall ads, covers, faces, and models is measured to determine what model connects best with the product. For beauty advertising, a face with good planes, high cheekbones, expressive eyes, good chin and hair is desirable. For print advertising, a model must be able to deliver the right expressions. If told you're a young lawyer going camping, the model has to understand what that entails and what's required. You are given simple direction – be frustrated, you're anxious and in pain, you're thrilled because this pharmaceutical product has revolutionized your life – the model must come across every time. The powers that be want to see evidence in your book or composite that you can do this type of assignment, and they may also ask you for an on the spot demonstration – what facial expression you would assume after three days of using Preparation H, for example.

Character types, grandmas, nerds, and every category imaginable are called for in print advertising. The model who can quickly become a virtual chameleon has the advantage. Starting in this category is hard because competition is keen; the money is good, so everybody is after the same work. A model may initially have no luck at first, and even a year later, people are still getting to know him or her. It takes time and perseverance. Photographers, casting people, ad agencies – all have to get accustomed to your being part of the scene. They want to observe over time how you react and what you can do. You, in turn, have to pick up on what advertisers want, even when they don't know themselves.

Publicity

Print publicity modeling can overlap with editorial, retail, wholesale and advertising, and in some cases with TV commercial modeling as well. Usually publicity modeling is a part of an overall campaign. Photos shot for publicity will be submitted to the media, to newspapers and magazines, which will hopefully find the press release newsworthy and thus feature it in its publication. Models are paid their hourly rates for publicity, unless they have an endorsement contract which covers this area as well.

Television commercials

The most extensive and exhaustive modeling go sees are for commercials. Commercials are a highly lucrative area; in fact, some models do no other work but commercials. Commercials can be great payers, sometimes bringing in several thousand dollars for a mere few hours in one partial day's work. Sometimes one commercial shoot can result in several spots which are edited for different markets, increasing exponentially the amount of compensation.

But landing a commercial is much more involved than getting a print job. Casting can sometimes continue for months, entailing several callbacks. Often a model has to prepare for auditions, sometimes with a script or monologue or with special clothing requirements.

The usual casting procedure is as follows: an agent sends out the model's glossy headshot for submission to casting directors, who do preliminary screening. Some screening is still done through advertising agencies' own casting departments, though most ad agencies now use outside casting people. Sometimes a couple of thousand models are involved in initial stages of the screening process, in which the best types and those head shots that arouse the most interest are chosen. Casting's initial choices will be passed on to the advertising agency, director and production house. Models who are deemed best for the parts will be called in to audition.

At the first live in-person casting call, usually a videotaped session, candidates are whittled down, with perhaps three or four dozen selected for another round of callbacks. These in turn are further narrowed to six or seven for final callbacks with the director.

The director reviews audition tapes, and candidates are then taped once again in the (hopefully) final callback session. Decisions are made by a committee consisting of the advertising agency (account executive, producer, art director, copywriter), production company (director and producer) and the client, if he is in town. If the client has not heretofore been present at any casting sessions, videotaped selections are sent to him digitally or via overnight Fed-Ex, or he flies in for a preproduction meeting, at which final selections are made. In all cases, the client makes the final decision, albeit with some coaching from the sidelines, with recommendations by others involved in the process.

The most sought after look for commercials is the general, all around middle American type, nice looking but not overwhelmingly so; next most requested types are character actors. For markets with a large retirement population, such as Florida and Arizona, older models are in demand.

TV casting requirements

What do casting people/ad agencies/clients look for when casting for a television commercial?

– Personality
– Enthusiasm, sparkle, energy
– Embodying the type required
– Reliability (being on time, being a pro, delivering the goods)

Models serious about succeeding in commercials should know:

– How to read copy
– How to direct their eyes to the camera
– How to convince the client you can sell the product.

Whom will you meet on a commercial audition?

– Casting director
– Director
– Producer
– Ad agency creative team (copywriter, art director, account executive)
– Client (sponsor)

What happens on a commercial interview?

When you go on a commercial interview, (always dressed for the part!), sign the sign- in sheet, give your name to the receptionist, and have your commercial headshot with you. You may be asked to leave it at the desk at sign-in, or to take it with you into casting. Additionally, a Polaroid may be snapped for reference.

You may be given a script or sides (lines) to look at, to be read on camera or not. You will be ushered into a back room, where you will meet anywhere from one to several persons. If you are auditioning on a sound stage or even in a business office, you could be asked to read lines or do other business while being videotaped.

You are paid union wages if you are detained over one hour, and for additional callbacks beyond the second one. You are also paid for any special business you are asked to do, such as improvisations, etc., or if you must supply a special wardrobe for the audition.

What happens in an on-camera audition?

You may be given details about the shoot, the character you are auditioning for, blocking, camera direction, or other special instructions. There will be a run-through and then the scene will be videotaped. The camera will roll, the scene will be slated, and you will go through your audition material, which may entail lines or simple reactions.

Sometimes you will be asked to make changes in your approach, to try things a different way. You may be asked questions about your credits and your availability; you might be asked to do an improv, either alone or with a partner.

When asked to do things they have never done before, some models feel foolish at first. With practice, you will be more comfortable (and even creative) trying your hand at anything you're asked to do. Sometimes spontaneity is all casting people are looking for – or they want to see your reactions. If something is asked of you that you feel awkward doing, don't worry - smile, laugh, crack a joke and be a good sport about it. The fact that you don't lose your cool and are willing to make an idiot of yourself is to your credit.

Keep in mind for commercials

When going on commercial auditions, your best move is to get to the audition early, so everyone who follows will be compared with you. This way, you set the curve. The first six people seen have the advantage; they make the initial impression. Remember that the early bird catches the worm.

Many models make the mistake of not dressing in character when going out for a commercial interview. Be sure you are appropriately dressed. If the job calls for a corporate type, don't go wearing a tank top with faded, cut off jeans and expect casting people to have the imagination that you'd look different in a suit and tie. You must dress exactly the way the part requires. Performers are given credit for their adhering to this rule.

If you have another go see following the corporate executive, one that calls for you to look like a street type, pack that pair of torn jeans together with the tank top in your tote and change for the second call. You want to make a favorable impression so that casting people in the future will remember you and request to see you for jobs coming up.

Project warmth. Talk with excitement and enthusiasm about your recent gigs, accomplishments and upcoming plans. Even if you've been inactive in terms of modeling jobs, think of something you're enthusiastic about to contribute to the back and forth chit chat: "I just returned from my sister's wedding in California – had an incredible time, but now it's back to business, and I'm ready!" "I just finished shooting my cat in an amazingly funny video that I uploaded to YouTube last night. I'm totally stoked about it, and so is the cat!"

Always appear to be leading an active life, even if you're not. One

74

of the most frequently asked questions a model encounters on go sees is, "What have you done?" and after people know you, "What have you been doing lately?" You cannot answer, "Nothing!" You must make your life sound successful and interesting. Even if your answer is just, "Taking classes," you have to make that activity appear important. Be excited about all your life's interests.

Present yourself as flexible, friendly, congenial, and cooperative. Sell yourself to the interviewer; refer to him by name. Always leave a composite.

Reading copy for commercials

In reading copy, keep in mind the five W's: Who are you? What are you doing? When are you doing it? Where are you doing it? Why are you doing it? Also ask yourself where have you just come from and what is your objective.

SAG-AFTRA, casting directors, and private teachers, many of whom advertise in trade papers and on the internet, offer classes in how to read for commercials. It is always a help to the beginning model to see copies of sample scripts and practice how to analyze copy. It is also an opportunity to make connections and network. Who knows, that casting director might call you in for a job next week or next month.

Scale, day rate or otherwise

TV commercial negotiations can be complex and involve many variables. Whether a model is paid SAG-AFTRA minimum or a higher rate depends on the model's strength, and the power of the agency to negotiate special rates. Many agencies representing print models will try to get the model's day rate applied to future residuals instead of settling for scale, because there is never any guarantee that a commercial will pay off; you seldom know in advance whether the commercial will go national or stay at test market level, in which case the pay would be less.

Residuals

A commercial that is played on television pays the model. known as the "principal," a royalty, known as a "residual." Residuals are complex in structure, with guidelines set by the union (SAG-AFTRA). The amount of residuals paid depends on whether your commercial runs in a Class A, B or C market, whether it is shown in prime time in New York, Los Angeles and Chicago, whether it is shown as a dealer spot, wild spot, or in other category, or all of the above.

Residuals are paid in 13 week cycles, You may receive payment for individual usage each time the commercial is aired nationally, or there may be a buyout price for the 13 week cycle. Spots (shown in between time slots) have one rate, program commercials another. Regional markets pay less than prime markets. You may have a combination of many markets. Based on union rules, the advertising agency tallies what amounts you are to be paid in residuals and writes the check. According to union rules, principals in commercials must be paid promptly or a penalty is charged.

Commercial pros and cons

Print can bring in $1500, $2000, $3000 a day or more, plus bonuses for usage, whereas most commercials technically pay only union day rate or scale, until residuals are assured; when one factors in the time spent auditioning and that the commercial may never run or may run only in low paying test markets, some commercials can end up being a disappointment.

There is a high conflict area in commercials; if you have done a commercial for one company, you are prevented from working on a comparable product for six months. This six month period can be extended to one year by another payment of the daily rate.

However, when a commercial goes national, it can be a cash cow, paying thousands, even hundreds of thousands of dollars (and more) in residuals. An added benefit is that everyone in the industry will be aware of your work.

A famous cereal commercial ("let Mikey taste it") ran for nine years, involving three child actors playing brothers at the breakfast table Those three boys each made over one million dollars apiece.

So what it boils down to is: models in commercials can make either peanuts or millions; commercials are unpredictable, but when you hit, you can hit big.

Who is present on a commercial shoot?

Crew members:

– Director

– Assistant Director (A.D.) – organizes and coordinates production, makes sure cast and crew are available when needed, advises cast when to assemble

– Cameraman, Assistant Cameraman

– Lighting Director

– Gaffers (electricians)

– Grips (move cameras and sets)

– Sound men (engineers)

– Prop men

– Greensmen (dress the set with flowers and plants);

– Script supervisor (times scenes, watches for matching);

– Hair, Makeup and Wardrobe people.

Commercial shoot guidelines

You are given your call, which will probably be anywhere from 5 to 8 a.m. if it's a morning call, as most are. You will probably be asked to report to the Assistant Director, unless you have a very early hairdressing call and the A.D. is not yet in. At any rate, the A.D. is the person you will be constantly in touch with all day; he must always know your whereabouts. Go to makeup, hair and wardrobe as you are advised, usually immediately. At some convenient time during the day, you will be asked to complete paperwork, fill out W4 forms, contracts, and so forth.

After hair, makeup, and wardrobe, you are ready to shoot. When the A.D. calls you on set, be prepared for a run through. The Director will probably show you the boards (story boards) and explain the action you are executing step by step. No doubt you have seen the script during auditions, and you may have a copy, but there may have been some late changes.

The Director will explain what he wants from you, the point, mood and tone of the situation to be filmed. When everyone, cast and crew alike, are ready, when the set has been lit, the crew is in place, your makeup, hair and wardrobe retouched and finalized, the A.D. will call, "Places." Following a successful run through, you will hear when the Director is ready to shoot. "Let's do a take." Everything quiets down on the set. The red light goes on above the sound stage door.

Each separate shot may require a dozen or more takes, some of which might be long shots, others closeups, but the majority in television are usually 3/4 shots, and in most setups, at least three or four takes are necessary.

You will be constantly starting, stopping, then starting over again until the Director is satisfied. Each time, you must get your energy level up to the original point, as the Director takes you back to what happened before, and the Script Supervisor advises on continuity – that is, everything must match: if in the previous shot you were holding a glass in your left hand and the clock behind you registered 10:30, in the next (matching) shot you can't hold the glass in your right hand and the clock can't read 11 (unless it's a new scene unrelated to the previous one).

The Director always brings you back to the quality he needs from you to sustain the action. Commercials are brief vignettes a few seconds in duration, very broad slices of life. Often the mood is one of humor and levity

Commercial must do's

Observe all instructions, such as "places," "quiet," "stand by," "roll," "slate it," "camera rolling," "speed," "action," "cut," "wrap," etc.

Know that scenes in commercials are usually not shot in sequence but that all scenes must match.

Always tell the A.D. where you're going, if you must leave the set.

Game shows

Another facet of television in which models can participate is live selling, exemplified by the game show, which combines the live modeling format with live television. Models in this category move objects, display merchandise, highlight winners' choices, usher in contestants to center stage, and so on. Most of these game show assignments are highly coveted because the work is steady and ongoing, and the models may remain as fixtures for years, in some cases over two and more decades, as was the case with the Mark Goodson Productions models. Game show models are hired through agencies covering work in live television.

Home Shopping Networks

Home Shopping Networks like HSN, QVC, Shop NBC and others hire models of all sizes, shapes, and ages, though women more than men are featured. It is not uncommon for plus models to be hired, as clothing manufacturers sell to this group, of which their viewers are many. You will often see women in their 70's with visible wrinkles chosen to model on the shopping channels, specifically because a product enhances the appearance of mature women as well as young ones. Occasionally, children may be needed.

Live selling and conventions

Models are used for live selling in trade and industrial shows, conventions, press conferences and sales meetings, luncheons, in hospitality suites, and at other similar events attended by the public.

Models who are good demonstrators can be important fixtures at such events; models can also disseminate flyers and product samples and handle motivational material. Models can be used for slide and film presentations at trade shows, or in industrial shows that are similar to live theatre. Often acting, singing or dancing talent is called for, in which case, often real people models and character people with acting experience are used for these assignments, with choices made through glossy photo submission followed by a round of auditions.

In many cases, working conditions at conventions are excellent, offering prime recreational values. Las Vegas conventions in particular are considered plum assignments. The Javits Center in New York, McCormack Center in Chicago, and the Los Angeles Staples Center are other popular ambiances for trade shows. Europe has a huge convention market, Paris and Milan being prime venues, but Germany, with eleven enormous convention centers called Messe, leads the pack.

Convention modeling may pertain to almost anything from fashion collections to electronics, housewares, gifts, and other consumer items. Some shows are multilingual; electronics shows often feature models speaking eight languages or more.

Models who work information booths must know the city, its attributes and facilities, and must be familiar with the general layout of the convention center itself. The model may frequently be required to give several product presentations a day. Many Detroit models started with the local auto shows, then branched out to advertising and commercial work in nearby Chicago and later New York and Los Angeles.

Models are chosen for trade convention work because of their superior salesmanship or their ability to understand a product function. In today's convention market, a more cultivated person is required than formerly, in order to attract upscale people to the booth who expect to be sold the product in a more educated manner. Some models are asked to explain the product to a potential buyer before turning the customer over to a salesman. In such cases, the model must be a good talker and a fast learner who can digest the company's information material after briefings.

To find work, models should align with an agency specializing in convention and live demonstration assignments. Fees in this category are lower than those paid for print and television commercials.

Length of assignments

Models may be booked for short periods of a day, two days, one or two weeks or more. Some conventions are traveling affairs visiting several different cities. Models may be chosen to come along for the entire itinerary, or separate talent may be hired in each individual city. On the city to city shows, some models are offered a year's contract, and may command up to $1000 a day and more.

The Garment Industry – wholesale, retail and runway

The apparel industry is a huge business worldwide, the major share of which is centered in New York, Paris, Milan, and London, as well as in Tokyo. If you're familiar with Manhattan, you probably know its historic Garment Center is located in a few blocks on the west side, roughly between 34th and 40th Streets between Fifth and Ninth Avenues.

But did you know that up until recently, the New York apparel industry was the #1 manufacturing sector in the United States, ahead of the auto industry? Did you know that, even with garment manufacturing jobs moving overseas, the New York apparel industry (also known as "the schmatte trade") is responsible for nearly 50 billion dollars of revenue per year, more than Paris and London combined?

All the major designers are here – Calvin Klein, Vera Wang, Michael Kors, Marc Jacob. The leading private labels for major stores are here as well, as are big businesses like Jones New York, Macy's, American Eagle, Liz Claiborne, Anne Klein, Nine West, and all the other famous names labels you undoubtedly wear, including private labels.

Fall and spring are the major collections, one week dressy clothes, the second week sportswear. Each major fashion center has designated times, collections beginning in Milan, the scene then shifting to London, Paris, and New York. Additional collections are shown in Tokyo, Rome, Florence, and in other, smaller markets. Top models work all major markets.

Runway models show garments in formal shows to wholesale buyers, who place orders for their stores; to the press corps which writes up the collections for their publications; and to key private buyers, such as celebrities and socialites.

Showings may be lavish productions, or they may be more low key; they can be solo shows or in conjunction with other designers.

Collections may be shown in a showroom, hotel ballroom, tent, with or without commentary, music and choreography. Major designers like to videotape their collections for later use in department stores. After the collections, garments are shown again in the designer's showroom on showroom models during market weeks, so the buyers can get a closer look.

After orders have been placed, garments are manufactured. Fitting models try on the garments, sizes are adjusted, final sizing decided. After the garments are shipped to the stores, in-store promotions begin and retail fashion shows are held. Designers or manufacturers may also have trunk shows traveling throughout the country at this point. Stores also offer models opportunities in informal modeling, where models circulate with customers on floors and in the store's restaurant.

New York has the greatest number of designers and wholesale manufacturers in the United States and is the largest market for showroom, fitting, and house models.

House models

Manufacturers who show their lines to visiting buyers need models to try on garments in their showrooms, particularly during market weeks, the industry's busiest seasons, which occur at least twice a year and sometimes four or even up to five times a year, depending on the designer's degree of activity. In-house modeling for designers can give a model valuable training and experience, and also help pay the bills while the model is waiting for the next rung of the ladder.

In-house modeling as stepping stone

Many models who went on to greater recognition started as house models in the garment industry. Lauren Bacall began as a David Crystal house model, replacing Lucille Ball and Dusty Anderson, was then discovered by fashion editors and ultimately by

Hollywood. Barbara Feldon got valuable ground training and paid the bills as a Claire McCardell house model, and went on to Revlon and "Get Smart" fame. Lauren Hutton and numerous others also paid their dues this way.

Market weeks

In market weeks, designers and manufacturers will hire additional models to supplement their full time house models. The two big seasons are the fall lines shown in April and spring lines in October. Every type clothing and accessories are shown during market weeks. A model showing bathing suits must be in good shape, including legs, feet, toes and bikini line.

If a model has exceptionally good legs and feet, she can join in the shoe and hosiery market. Swim wear is followed by the fur market; there's the lingerie market too, as well as the large and petite markets. Petites show shoes well because they usually have small feet.

Work can involve evenings and weekends during season, and busy models can handle several separate assignments in one day. Models in this venue usually have to do their own hair and makeup.

If you're working this market freelance and are hired on an "outs" basis, you can get time off to slip in other bookings and go-sees. Additionally, if there's a major show for a department store, the model can be put into that for an hour or so and then go back to her showroom.

Other cities in the US, such as Los Angeles, Dallas, Chicago, and Atlanta, all have large merchandise marts and are good places for a model to apply for employment. Although the secondary, regional markets are not as active as New York, they nevertheless provide invaluable training.

Many models also do this type of work abroad, especially in Italy, which not only has Milan as its pinnacle, but a wide range of secondary designer markets, including Rome, Florence, Bari, Ancona, and others.

Fitting models

Designers need models for "writing appointments" (sessions with buyers who write the orders). Two types of fitting models are used: one fits the sample, the other does the duplicate pattern fittings that end up going into production. Production patterns are sized larger. A model needs perfect measurements for the garment, which vary from manufacturer and market. Sizing often depends on whether the garments are from a designer line or budget line – the latter fit bigger by one or more inches at the bust, waist and hips: a designer size 8 becomes a 10 in budget, and so on.

A fit model has to know what's wrong with a garment, where it pulls or bunches and how it feels to wear. A fitting model isn't just a pretty face or a mere clothes hanger; she has to not only know how to wear clothes and present them with style, but how to enhance them and make them come alive.

Fitting for a designer is a multi-step process, going from paper to muslin to finished garment, entailing five or six fittings, noting changes from one stage to another. Fittings for samples as well as production garments involve quality control in which buttons are placed and replaced, lapels checked for width and shape, for laying flat or rolled. Garments must be in exactly the right proportions and every detail must be correct. Involving the model at early stages of garment creation is considered an advantage to the designer.

Obtaining a job as an in-house model

The usual procedure is for a model to visit the major showrooms, where the manager will ask her to try on three or four garments. If they like her personality, the way she moves and the way the garments fit, they will book her when they have an opening. She can expect to earn between $200-$275 an hour or more, or between $750-$1500 a day and up.

Working in a merchandise mart or especially in a large apparel industry like New York's Seventh Avenue, a model can network easily and meet new clients. In time, she will be booked by other manufacturers as well as department stores, and she may even break into photography if she does the designer collections.

Collection fitting

Collection fitting involves many hours of patience being on one's feet. A garment is begun on the model by draping muslin and pinning it together; next comes a sized pattern, then an original sample. Each fabric is individual and reacts differently, depending on whether the garment is bias, straight, flat, gathered, or whatever. A good model has an instinct for how clothes are draped, for what works and what doesn't. In the course of her engagements, the model learns a great deal not only about how different designers feel about clothes, but also about production. Some dresses turn out too expensive to manufacture; others don't wear well. The model can help the designer to discover these important things.

The model is an integral part of both the excitement and the pressure surrounding collection time fashion shows. Some in house models are used, and supplemented with models booked on a free lance basis. A free lancer in this category can jump from showroom to showroom, showing shoes, furs, sportswear, coats, swim wear, outerwear, and so on, all of which are separate markets with individual buying seasons. Each month a new market hits town, with work available two weeks in each market. During market week, buyers come in from all areas of the country to scout lines.

In New York, 550, 530, and 498 Seventh Avenue as well as 1430 Broadway are headquarters to a tremendous variety of showrooms featuring every type of apparel imaginable, and the model who knocks on doors here will find a wealth of opportunity for work.

Writing appointments

Following designer showings, different showrooms will stage informal, private showings of perhaps two or three hours in duration, with as many as six models showing the line to important buyers who either want a second look or were unable to make the opening. These could be retail customers, the press, foreign editors, or important clients from society and show business. These sessions are given as an opportunity to place orders.

Models showing at this time won't wear the entire collection but a capsulized version of it. These sessions are less formal than runway presentations but more so than presentation at a department store.

Models who show in different categories learn how to adapt their look and attitude in order to present the clothes to their best advantage. For instance, furs have to be made to look longer, thicker and richer; they demand more makeup and the assumption of a more sophisticated look.

Trunk shows

Designer clothing is modeled at suburban malls and in department stores across the nation, for which designers need models. Usually, once a designer is satisfied with a model, he will book and rebook her or him.

Designers take road trips, and some models are hired to go with them. A designer and his entourage may travel to ten cities in twelve days, visiting New York three or four times in the process. A designer wants a model who projects the designer's attitude into each article of clothing. Sometimes the model is called upon to incorporate objects on stage as well, by reacting and interacting with props and other features of the collection.

A model must instinctively know when to pause and stand still for a few seconds, when to turn and when not to, and how to remain cool under pressure. She or he should intuitively grasp when to keep one hand in a pocket or spread out the lining of a fur, when to remove outerwear, when to unbutton or to button; she/he must be on top of subtleties such as where to turn or stop, and when and how to recognize key figures in the audience.

Sometimes designers who bring their collections to a regional area will book local models to supplement their regulars.

Department stores

Along with high profile models, designers have become increasingly recognized and publicized today more than ever. One of the most important outlets designers rely on to enhance their careers are department stores, many of which offer prestige and often an exclusive image to the designer.

Image is important to a department store as well, because many other chains may carry the identical clothing; thus model selection is crucial to emphasize the store's particular brand. Merchants want to emphasize the image they are trying to project to the customer – the customer must know instantly she's looking at that store's catalog or ad. Bloomingdale's should never be confused with Macy's or Sears with J.C. Penney. If a model works for too many competing stores, the store will drop her/him and hire other models instead.

The best way to enter retail modeling is through the wholesale route, by working for a designer. Retail can be a good springboard to other things, as it is a virtually unlimited market. Even small stores need models. Regional department stores comprise a big market, and are a perfect place to gain experience. Many models began this way, especially those not living near a major market. Celebrity model (and Academy Award nominated actress) Andie

McDowell started in a department store in her native South: "I just went down to a department store and asked them if I could model," says Andie.

Regional department stores provide a valuable training ground, as it is increasingly difficult for a young model to come to New York and make it straight away in the retail market without prior experience elsewhere.

Additional opportunities in department store modeling

For store mailing pieces, catalogs and newspaper advertising, the store's creative department looks over the merchandise, decides what photographer will shoot, where, and whom. They call a model agency to book specific models they have worked with in the past, and are also receptive to seeing new models.

Stores also use live in-store floor models. Makeup, fragrance and other demonstrations and promotion models may hand out literature, engage customers in conversation, or participate in live demonstrations and promos. Be prepared – it can be exhausting to be on one's feet for hours at a stretch.

Stores feature informal modeling, and hire models for tearoom showings, casual modeling walking around the store, among aisles and tables, showing clothing to guests and diners, answering questions. For this work, a pleasant, outgoing personality is required. Stores also feature charity previews, which usually involve quick changes.

Some specialty departments hire house models who work on the floor in a particular department, usually one carrying high priced clothing like furs, designer dresses, formal wear or bridal gowns.

At times, department stores will feature special events, coordinated shows for the entire chain.

Runway

Runway modeling came into its own toward the end of the 20th century, when it became dominated by international models with a high recognition factor, some of whom were larger than life figures. Once held to be less important than other types of modeling, the prestige associated with runway began in the late 70's to early 80's, evolving from the days of Jerry Hall, Imam and Pat Cleveland to the days of Naomi Campbell, Tyra Banks, Claudia Schiffer, Veronica Webb, Linda Evangelista, Carla Bruni, Cristy Turlington, Kate Moss, Frederique and Stephanie Seymour to the "now" list of catwalkers with names like Karlie Kloss, Anja Rubik, Natasha Poly, Karmen Pedaru, Anna Jagodzinska, Jac Jagaciak, Theres Aledandersson, Daphne Groeneveld, Melodie Monrose, Iris Egbers, Melodie Kulicka, and Marcelia Freesz

What does it take to be a runway model?

A runway model has the ability to carry himself/herself with flair and the authority to look poised and self-assured. A runway model must be aware of which garment details to show, how and when to focus where – on lifting a collar, calling attention to a hemline; how to make a garment flow, how to move compellingly, and how to sell the clothes.

Every garment has a better side, and it is the model who reveals that to the customer. In showing layered clothing, a model must remove each item gracefully and differently. Once removed, the garment must be retained – tied at the waist, draped on a shoulder, pulled over the arm. Each step becomes a decision according to the clothes and the model's imagination.

A model must know how to cope with all types of clothing, long trains, short tight skirts, bathing suits and bridal gowns. She must be able to walk gracefully under difficult conditions in uncomfortable shoes on different sizes and shapes of runways that have different surfaces – tile, carpet, polished wood, etc.

Every show has a purpose, and the model has to embody this. The entrance initiates a show's tone. As he/she sashays on the catwalk, a model can instinctively feel how pacing is set by accompanying music, and, with practice and experience, it becomes second nature to project the attitude called for. Each turn, each pass must be within the character called for by the designer, the music's tempo, lighting effects and theatrical devices.

The runway model masters the casual smile, the fast paced yet natural, authoritative walk, perfectly timed in correct rhythm. The model is ever alert to the starter who is giving directions backstage. There is no room for clumsiness; all is precision.

Runway check list

– All turns should be toward the audience.

– Never leave a runway vacant.

– Always walk on the same side to avoid collisions.

– When you reach the end of the runway, allow photographers to shoot the garment from all angles.

– Whether choreographed or not, runway is performance at its height, theatrical spectacles of light, sound, and color, timed to perfection. Runway modeling comes with a whole support crew – set designers, choreographers, sound engineers.

– Runway modeling can be done in groups, as tableaux and/or statues or other formation. Usually a model is not alone on the runway.

– Attitude and energy are the thrusts of a runway model's technique. Either instinctively or through imitation and practice, the model has the head and shoulder movements, the basic turns, the walk, and how to act on the runway down pat. The charge has to come from within. Imagination is required to change moods to suit the outfit. You are always selling clothes. It's your job to make the audience want those clothes, and to make it fun. Gestures add to the total impact. The model is on display, and must create attention with charisma and style, she/he must make an impact and suit the client's image.

Pointers for runway models

– Watch models on DVDs, television, and YouTube to learn from their styles.

– Work the clothes

– Each runway – wood, tile, carpet, cloth-covered, or other – requires adjustments.

– Shoes may be difficult to walk in and may be taped; walking up and downstairs can take practice.

– Keep your approach, turn, and exit smooth; when turning, keep your eyes on the audience.

– Master quarter turns, pivots, swings, full and half turns, one and a half turns, the bridal turn; practice removing coats and jackets, opening buttons, swinging garments over the shoulder, dragging garments, placing hands in pockets, on hips; handling handbags and other props such as tennis racquets, golf clubs, beach towels also takes experimenting and practice.

– Gesturing: some movements go in and out of style; check and be sure you are up to date.

– Use expressions that suit the garments, sophisticated for evening wear, casual and open for sportswear; take on the character of the garment.

– Be alert to how the garment moves, to special instructions, and to any choreography to be memorized.

Runway guidelines

– Doubles, groups split the runway

– Runways may be t shaped, u shaped, in the round, of varying heights, shapes, lengths, and materials.

– Photographers may be present or not; if so, you must know precisely where to pose and how.

– Quick changes are required.

People you will encounter in a runway show

Designer, show coordinator, dresser, fitter, checker, starter, and presser.

CHAPTER 5 – A MODEL NEEDS TO KNOW

Booking information

Pre-booking information consists of the who, what, when, where, why and how of a modeling assignment. You must know the client's and product's name, the time and location of the booking, the name and title of the person you are to report to (Assistant Director, Studio Manager, etc.), and what type job you are booked for (print, TV, Runway, etc.).

Additionally, you must know if the job is a weather permit, what is the wardrobe information, and if you are to bring anything to the booking, (clothing, shoes, accessories). Furthermore, will there be a makeup artist? Hairdresser? Stylist?

Other questions the model needs to know: are there any pre-booking appointments to be kept? Do you have to show wardrobe ahead of time? Is there a pre-booking fitting (for which you are paid) involved? If so, what is the fee? If you must bring something specific out of the ordinary for the shooting for which there is no stylist to provide, you may be given an extra payment, usually half your hourly rate.

For the booking itself, will you be given an hourly rate, a daily rate, union minimum, a buyout? If this is a commercial, is it known whether it will test market or go into major markets? When will it start to run?

Some bookings are arranged months in advance, with holds that may be canceled close to the wire; other bookings are tentative with an option to cancel. If a model gets busy on another assignment and must cancel a tentative booking, a new model may be booked at the last minute to fill the job.

Fittings

If you have brought your own clothing, show all items to the stylist and/or photographer or client or whatever person is in charge of wardrobe decision making. (Choosing wardrobe may be a joint effort). You may be asked to try on the clothing, in which case you should wear and show the garments as if you are in a modified fashion setting.

Vouchers

For print assignments, models turn in vouchers. The voucher system was initiated by A&P heir Huntington Hartford, who founded the Hartford Agency in the 1940's. Prior to then, models often had to wait long periods of time before receiving payment. Thanks to the voucher system, models are paid almost immediately for a job, even if the client has not paid. Most agencies pay on a weekly or biweekly basis. Vouchers are signed in triplicate, one for the client, one for the agency and one for the model.

Agency commissions and affiliations

Most agencies receive a 20% commission from models on print jobs, and a 20% service fee from the client. New models may be asked for 25% until they are established. On commercials, agencies take 10%. In most states, agencies must be licensed and bonded; those working in television must also be union franchised (by SAG-AFTRA). Additionally, if they represent actors in plays, they must be franchised by Actors' Equity Association, and if they represent variety artists who perform in cabarets and nightclubs, they must be franchised by AGVA (American Guild of Variety Artists).

Agency guidelines are set by IMMA (International Model Managers Association). To belong, an agent must be established as a model manager, be on the voucher system, have a head sheet, and be in business for over a year.

Sample model rates

Advertising bookings are the highest paid individually, though TV commercials can add up to more money in the long run, depending on the markets the commercial runs in. Catalog, the bread and butter of modeling, pays a good hourly or daily rate which is worthwhile when the work is steady. A model's advertising rate is double or triple his catalog rate.

Fashion shows employing supermodels was known in the past to have paid as much as $20,000 per booking. Supermodel Naomi Campbell hit the news several years back when she demanded a pay increase, $35,000 for a runway appearance. When the client refused, Naomi had to settle for her customary rate of $20,000 – still nice work if you can get it. But probably you can't get it anymore. Runway rates today may run only 5-10% of what they were at the height of the supermodel craze.

Some fashion shows pay a regular hourly or daily rate, others pay a flat fee. Amounts vary widely. It has also been suggested that some of the exorbitant modeling fees are inflated for the sake of publicity. Certain designers are said to have balked at the high charges of the supermodels and a backlash occurred, in which designers made it known that other models possess many of the same abilities and charisma as the superstars, but cost less, thus, designers threatened to jump ship and abandon the supermodels, which apparently became a fait accompli.

Model editorial rates are established by magazines and are low. Editorial assignments are not done for the money but for prestige, exposure and career enhancement.

SAG-AFTRA payments

Commercials, union scale: In addition to being paid a daily rate for shooting a commercial, a model may also either be paid on a buyout basis (in which the fee covers any and all usage over a 13 week period) or be paid individually each time the commercial is aired. Payment is based on complex criteria regulated by the union, established by the markets the commercial runs in.

Overtime, TV commercials: Over 8 hours, the first additional two hours are paid at time and a half, after that double time. Saturday, Sunday and holidays are double time.

Overtime is paid at the rate of time and a half after 5:30 pm; double time is paid after two hours overtime for union members in television and film jobs.

Travel time is paid for if the model is required to go outside the studio zone or to a radius of a certain number of miles away from the city.

Wardrobe, Commercials: The model is paid the union rate for wardrobe calls. If the model supplies his own clothes he is paid a union established amount for each item worn during the shoot.

Holding Fees: A model cannot accept a conflict over the 13 week period following the shoot. The client can buy out the contract an additional 13 week period without using it by paying another session fee.

For union jobs, contracts are signed, W4 forms filled out each time; vouchers are not used.

Rehearsals: Half hourly rate

Formal wear: A cleaning fee is provided per garment

Buyouts are for 13 week periods.

Other contingencies include shopping fees (if you must buy something out of the ordinary for a job); weather permits, cancellations, travel time, overtime, penalties. Check with the union for specifics.

Print Payments

Weather Permits: Usually, the model is asked to phone in a couple of hours prior to scheduling, to see if the job is on or not. There is a fee charged for weather permits, one half the regular fee, and the job is rescheduled. If there is another weather permit cancellation, the model receives a full fee.

Cancellations: bookings involve a cancellation fee if the client is the one to cancel. The client can cancel up to two working days prior to the booking without a penalty. If the booking is canceled with less than 48 hours' notice, the model is paid one half of the amount he/she would have made on the booking. If the job is canceled less than 24 hours before the booking, the model is paid in full.

Some agencies enforce even stricter rules and require a week's notice on cancellations with penalties enforced, and will charge the full fee for a job that is canceled 72 hours prior to original scheduling.

If a job is finished ahead of schedule, a fee close to the full fee is charged.

Fittings for photography sessions: Hourly rate is calculated at half hour increments

Lingerie: Double hourly rate for undergarments, rate and a half for nightgowns, etc.

Some booking fees are established by the client, such as magazine editorial.

Exclusive contracts and product endorsements are negotiated, and often involve seven figure payments.

If a picture appears simultaneously in different areas such as print advertising, point of sale, billboard, packaging, or brochures, an appropriate usage fee is negotiated which can amount to several thousand dollars.

Celebrity Models receive higher fees because of their high visibility. For this reason, many models employ P.R. to keep their names before the public, to enhance their image.

Booking out

If you must be out of town or are for any reason unavailable to work, you must call the agency as far ahead of time as possible and let them know so they can "book you out," i.e., make it known you are unavailable during that period.

Whom do you see?

Wholesale fashion work means seeing the designer or the showroom supervisor. For traveling runway shows, you should see the manufacturer's rep. On photo assignments, you see the fashion editor, photographer or his assistant, the stylist or studio manager. These people will select from a collection of submitted pictures. In commercial print, the ad agency will assemble a file, and you will be called in if you are the type they're looking for. Casting directors are the initial screeners for commercials.

Be sure to write down what the client said on all your interviews; follow up. If you are told something is coming up you are right for, let your agent/booker know, and follow up with a later phone call.

You and your Booker

Especially when you are getting started in modeling, you need to rely on your booker's expert advice for everything. Modeling depends on contacts, connections, networking, getting to know people, making them aware of who you are and what you can do.

Someone has to feel responsible for your career, and for many fashion models, the person who fills this role is their booker.

Large agencies have several bookers, each of whom is assigned to service a certain group of models, perhaps ten in number, depending. It is the booker's job to manage the model's schedule and to know where that model is at all times. Initially, your booker will inform you of the agency's booking policy, procedures, and rates on weather permits, overtime, cancellations, minimums, and other needed facts you will have to know when you are booked for assignments.

Bookers are the link between the model and client; they prearrange all appointments and rounds. Your booker will have your schedule of go sees, auditions, callbacks, fittings, tests, jobs interviews, bookings, and other appointments. She sets up look sees with photographers, editors, stylists, hairdressers, and makeup artists while the model is on the testing board, and handles all booking offers and cancellations after the model is established. It's her job to leave enough time between appointments for contingencies. When one model has to cancel, or if a model requested for a specific job is unavailable, the booker can suggest a substitute, thus offering new models a chance to work. Sometimes last minute bookings are arranged on the spur of the moment, and a model who is ready to step in can pick up bookings as a result, so you should maintain frequent contact with your booker in case something like this comes up.

Your booker will see to it that your pictures are sent to prospective clients on its mailing and go see lists; arrange for models to meet with prospective clients, and supervise updating portfolios. In some cases the booker negotiates contracts, and in all cases will look for feedback.

Your booker is the person you will deal with at the agency whenever there's a problem. If you're detained, if you have a conflict, if any misunderstanding arises on set, or if you have changed anything about your appearance, your booker is the first person you must inform. The booker gets you out of tight spots, acts as buffer, fall guy, and heavy. If the booking is running overtime and you are desperate to get somewhere else, you don't handle it with the client, the booker does.

Models check in with their bookers a few times a day to get updates and last minute changes. A booker screens calls that come through the agency. Whenever a model has to book out, that is, when the model is unavailable for work, the booker is the first to be informed. An agency should always be able to find a model within the hour.

Many bookers become friends with the models they are in charge of and see them socially; models will invite their bookers to dinner and offer gestures like gifts and theatre tickets. In fact, there are models who regard their booker as a cross between sibling, psychiatrist, relationship counselor, baby sitter, banker, accountant and detective. Leading agencies can book a model all over the world.

Your booker will advise you on any and all in sundry matters, including the all-important subject of your test photos and what photographers are best suited for your type. At the same time, you should start to develop your own judgment in this direction as well.

CHAPTER 6 - MODELING NICHES

Superstars & Supermodels

Modeling offers career opportunities to virtually every type, but only a very small, select group become superstars and supermodels. These models are super-achievers at the very pinnacle of the modeling field, whose work is highly visible in runway, fashion editorial, beauty ads, television commercials, posters, billboards and calendars; they strut their stuff in haute couture gowns costing as much as $300,000 and more, and endorse products for which they are paid well into the seven figures. These models must be young, tall, thin, photogenic, charismatic, and promotable.

A model who is actively earning $250,000 - $750,000 a year (as was Cindy Crawford at one time in her modeling career) faces the test of how to reach the next level, where she can earn millions. Elite's Monique Pillard masterminded such a move for Cindy with posters, calendars, Sports Illustrated assignments, and by building product identification.

It was Pillard who envisioned a sexy angle and started models doing quasi-nudes, a variation of the old pinup/ cheesecake theme that had not previously been done by girls of this caliber, although it had been widely seen in Europe for years. A whole new American style evolved, a non-fashion image that was borderline risqué, once reserved for tarts and nudies, but done with artful photography shot by top, prestigious photographers. It created a sensation and made the models in this category into celebrities.

Modeling can be a stepping stone into manufacturing, design, the entertainment arts, politics, and other areas, as many models, both male and female, have proven. A model didn't used to be able to continue posing beyond a certain point in time, but today, a number of enduring celebrity models are still in demand. All have proven that the modeling image can be sustained into the 40's, 50's,

60's and beyond, and that a model can still be as glamorous as ever in her more mature years.

Of the thousands of modeling applicants each year, only a handful are selected for training by agencies, and out of this group just a minuscule percentage, the crème de la crème, become supermodels. Those with potential to reach the top are signed, nurtured and groomed. Increasingly, agencies are also taking young men under their wings, grooming them in a manner once reserved only for female models.

Though those who arrive at the rarified apex of modeling may be few and far between, but there is more than enough room in the industry for lesser lights, and an abundance of money to be made by all ages and types of both sexes.

Models other than supermodels must be more resourceful, however, particularly at the outset of their careers. Non-supermodels, including children and character people, have to foot their own bills, pay for their own pictures, wardrobe, makeup, hairdressers, classes, dentists and a host of other items to get their careers jump started.

Male models

Male models have come far over the past number of years. Once seen as little more than props or incidentals, men have moved onto the runway in a major way, assumed star/celebrity supermodel status, and now enjoy tremendous visibility in the industry.

The man most responsible for this phenomenon is British-born David Bosman, founder of Boss Models, Inc., who saw the niche in male models and went for it. Today, Boss is one of the most respected and successful agencies in the business, considered innovators who have forever altered the modeling landscape.

Says Jason Kanner, Soul Model Management: "Male models are as big as their female counterparts, which is a radical change. Instead of just looking, people want to get to know who these men are."

David Bosman again: "Men's fashion now says it's acceptable to be a little vain, and heterosexual men, like heterosexual women, use magazines to collect as much information as they can about how they can look – and that's where the models come in."

A former male model himself, Bosman confides, "I always had a huge interest in fashion, particularly the universe of men's fashion, since my early teens ... the presentation of gentlemen has always intrigued me." He remembers watching "Cary Grant in his crisp white shirts, and the simplicity of Steve McQueen in his hush puppies – their mannerisms, their etiquette, their presence. It wasn't about what they wore; it was about who they were. The detail was everything to me. We try to apply this same detail to the top level supermodels Boss represents today, Detail is second nature in the menswear field and in the minds of the models I represent."

When he considers American men, Bosman thinks of "the smart but casually practical clothing of America. On a more traditional and formal level, like the tailoring and bespoke couture of Saville Row, there could be nothing finer than the Duke of Windsor in a Price of Wales double-breasted suit."

All of these, says Bosman, comprise elements of men's style, "combined today with a greater awareness of one's own body and self..."

Male models undergo the same development process as women, but it generally takes a man longer to get established; the momentum is tougher to build and initially it can be discouraging for men, who seem to take rejection harder than women. Says a busy male model, "The one thing you need to be successful as a model is the one thing you have no control over... but it's a pretty charmed life," he admits.

Indeed, it takes a certain personality to tolerate the negatives of the profession – not only rejection, but the poking and prodding, working in close quarters, being ordered to put this on, take that off, stand thus and so, don't move. The passiveness of waiting to get picked, the temporary aspect modeling represents, the never ending rounds and testing for months without a payoff goes against the grain and the male ego. Getting known by key people requires effort, and a model can be a long time testing and developing a book and a look.

What kind of men become male models? Male models come from all walks of life and from every corner of the globe. "Fashion is about lifestyle as much as clothes. People are increasingly looking for personality in models. Long gone are the chisel-jawed dumb idiots."

Women can change their hair and makeup, can manage to vary their image and appear different in each photo, but men are more limited. On the other hand, men have some advantages – their career can begin later than women's and their look can evolve into a desirable brand of maturity over a period of time. Men seem to age better, in that a few wrinkles bring out their character and make them more interesting, whereas this is not usually the case with women. A woman who is beautiful when young usually does not age naturally into a character woman, but tends to cling to the early glamour, which is a much more difficult thing to pull off past a certain age.

A good haircut, some basic clothes and an attitude, and a man is ready for testing. He might take six months or more to develop, or he might get his first booking and start to take off almost immediately, sometimes using just one or two shots to sell himself. As much as women, men rely on the mentor, agency, and photographer to get rolling and keep a career moving.

Unlike women, men can continue modeling for an extended time. Age 40 can be a great point for a man. Some male models are hitting their stride at 50 and even 60 or more, depending on their look and market.

How do men break into the business?

By and large, methods are similar for men and women – being interviewed, getting an agency behind you, building a portfolio and client list through testing, go sees, auditions, and establishing a reputation through exposure. A man may be discovered or he may seek out the business himself.

Some agencies and photographers scout for men. Japanese photographers go to Los Angeles or Seattle to look for male models; men can be found right off the beaches and sent to Germany and Japan. Japan also has a lot of TV commercial work for Caucasian male models, as well as fashion and advertising.

Some men get into the profession through accident, a fluke, on a dare, or almost as a joke. An amazing number were spotted in malls across the country.

What qualities does a man need to model?

The male model must be photogenic. It helps to have prominent cheekbones, a well defined jaw line, and facial planes flattered by light. For fashion, a 40 regular suit is ideal (minor alterations ok); the man should have an elongated middle, broad shoulders, and good proportions, ideally a 32 waist, 10 inch rise, 40-42 chest, 15 ½ neck, 33 sleeve. He should be between 6 feet and 6'2" tall and weigh approximately 170 pounds. Preferably a man should be considered on the handsome side, rugged, and not too pretty, although this look varies with the times to include other types. For television commercials and print advertising, most requirements do not apply, as any size, height and weight can be needed, type being the criterion in each case.

"If we believe in this guy, we keep pushing and experimenting," says one male model agent. "We start moving the man right away, as soon as he arrives in town, we send him to the catalog studios, production houses, and photographers. We get behind him and don't give up till he's on top."

What type modeling assignments do men do?

Men can do everything women can!

Men appear in television, fashion editorial, runway, advertising print and catalog, wholesale and retail modeling, in most of the same capacities as their female counterparts. Men are prominently featured in cars, liquor, cologne and aftershave, airlines, hair care, fast food and cigarette ads; they receive lucrative fragrance and designer contracts, the same as women.

50% of all ads feature men along with women. Men appear in pinup calendars, and are used by department stores, clothing manufacturers and catalog houses, modeling formal attire and business suits, shirts, bathing trunks, and any other kind of menswear apparel. In time, male models acquire a sense of clothes, and a seasoned male model will be in demand to work for Japanese and Euro designers as well as in the American markets.

Male Models are used on a regular basis by high profile clients such as Donna Karan, Estée Lauder, Banana Republic, L'Oreal, Revlon, Tommy Hilfiger, Ralph Lauren, Calvin Klein, Versace, GQ, Vanity Fair, Harper's Bazaar, Vogue, L'Uomo Vogue, Vogue Homes, Elle, Marie-Claire, and many, many others.

What male model type is in demand?

Every type of male model is used, from the Ivy Leaguer in Brooks Brothers suit and rep tie, gay, macho, geek, baby boomer conservative, young father to business executive with a corporate image. Other popular categories are student, junior executive, older father, and retiree. The semi-nerd with glasses as well as unshaven, greasy haired looks are also in demand. However, the male fashion model is kept busiest. Male models are no longer predominantly gay, as was once the case, but there is plenty of room for gay types as well as straights. The profession is respected, considered a very masculine, even macho one today.

As with women, men too are used as fitting models. Men who fit for designers must learn patience. They are told to when to sit and stand, asked how does it feel, where does it grab, how is the pocket placement, the length. Every part of garment is assessed and adjusted, and the man is expected to make a contribution by voicing his opinions.

As with women, male models fit in muslin and after that in fabric. If the same design is to be used for a specific pant, it is fitted in each separate fabric – worsted, linen, cotton, corduroy, and so forth. Different adjustments are needed for each – some fabrics stretch more, and some garments don't feel the same even if they are sized the same. Men fit for outerwear, tuxedos, suits, jackets, blazers, slacks, shirts, sweaters, underwear, and every other conceivable type of apparel.

"The coolest thing about being a guy model is the money, pretty girls, traveling and a flexible schedule," says one in demand male model. "The worst thing is not knowing how long your success will last."

Modeling and beyond for men

Many men move to Europe and stay there for extended periods. They may initially be sent on an assignment, or go on spec or because their mother agency thinks European exposure is a good idea.

Men often learn the ropes from other models about which agencies and cities to try when. They can work all the world capitals plus secondary markets like Amsterdam, Belgium, Barcelona, Madrid, and particularly the smaller cities of Italy, a country which is very sophisticated and fashion oriented, and where fashion houses exist in secondary cities like Bari, Bologna, Ravenna, Ancona, Florence, and Verona. A man who does rounds all over the world will establish himself and be fed into smaller markets; clients will call him back when they have work. "Once you know your way around, it's easy to hit all the shows," one male model says.

Men take the business seriously, diet, work out, and exercise daily. Most of them want to make a lot of money and see the world.

David Bosman sums up

David Bosman comments on what we are experiencing in men's fashion today: " ... Levi jeans with a bespoke jacket, a fabulous haircut, or indeed, no haircut... throw in some wraparound glasses, a cell phone and an iPad, and you have the gentleman of the future.

"Of course, the exterior is only one element of what really makes a gentleman, or indeed a supermodel. There are other aspects – discipline, timing, travel, and most importantly, a sensitivity and understanding of the photographers and artists with whom they work. Without the artists in our industry, none of these images and aspirations could be seen.

"There is an aspect of the industry that requires time, precision, detail and intellect. The administrators of these aspects are what we call ... agents. An agent is capable of bringing together an artist from one country, a photographer from another, a client from a separate continent and a designer who is out of this world to combine their talent and watch something evolve into everything."

Children

Some child models start modeling almost as soon as they are born.. It's never too early to start. Many well known actors and actresses today started their careers as child models and kept going to the top.

Twins, triplets and other multiples are desirable in shoots using babies and young children, due to work restrictions whereby youngsters may not work beyond a set time. Casting directors will frequently wish to cast parts for 14-17 year olds using an 18 year old, because of child labor laws.

The Professional Children's School, New York City

To make it easy for child performers to meet professional commitments while pursuing an academic program suited to their special needs, the world famous Professional Children's School in Manhattan was founded during the early part of the 20th century. Some of the most famous names in modeling, theatre, film, music, dance and allied professions are PCS graduates: Milton Berle, Beverly Sills, Sidney Lumet, Marvin Hamlisch, Yo Yo Ma, Midori, Leslie Uggams, Leslie Ann Warren, Jerry O'Connor, Christopher Walken, Christian Slater, Donald Phaisan, Tara Reid, Scarlett Johansen, Martha Plimpton, Ricki Lake, Carrie Fisher, the "Cosby Kids" – the list is endless.

Most clients in New York, especially those who deal with SAG and AFTRA, will schedule kids' go sees after school hours. Those youngsters working on a film or television show locally, of course, are subject to normal calls and will have to be absent from school. At these times, as well as when children are called out of town on assignments, PCS allows them to go on correspondence.

"We have a special situation with models," says Carol Kleban, Professional Children's School's Principal. "The priorities of academics conflict much more with the priorities of modeling than with other branches of the performing arts. Unlike SAG-AFTRA jobs, modeling go sees are often scheduled at any hour of the day, during school hours, which makes it difficult for a student who is modeling to do his class work properly."

The above illustrates the conflicting priorities young models who have not yet finished their schooling may face in the profession.

Character People

Most character people know they're in it for the long haul. They acclimate quickly, realizing that to advance their careers, optimally they belong either in New York or Hollywood, preferably both, in which case they are bi-coastal. Sometimes they will share dual-coast apartments with other actors, so that there will always be a place to stay when the job calls for it on either coast. They make rounds in similar fashion to models, concentrating not so much on photographers (unless they are model types able to supplement their acting income), but on talent agents, casting directors, and other personnel connected with stage, screen, and television.

They are wise to enroll in high profile acting classes that give the chance of networking with their peers who may be future stars in a position to hire them later on, as well as with teachers who will be supportive and perhaps even suggest them for upcoming roles. They know the value of being prepared for auditions, of cultivating as many skills as possible, and making their presence known through publicity in as many areas as possible. Once they have landed significant work, it's time for the big P.R. splash, which they will make the most of.

CHAPTER 7 - MAKEUP AND HAIRSTYLING

Makeup for different media varies. Makeup used in photographic modeling is unlike street makeup, and the makeup you use for still photography will differ from your stage or commercial modeling makeup. High fashion makeup is more sophisticated, beauty and cosmetics done to suit the image of the company; runway makeup is extreme, more theatrical than most photographic makeup, even though the model is photographed at the end of her run.

For professional work in general, you need more base than you use for street wear, and various other factors will vary as well. In fashion and advertising print, professional makeup artists are employed, budget permitting. In television, often you are photographed from the waist up, looking fairly natural, but the makeup may be heavy panstick or pancake, because of the bright lights. This is not your concern. Makeup professionals will apply whatever is recommended, not you; almost all television commercials use makeup artists, and many also have a hairstylist. Nevertheless, models should know how to do their own makeup and hairstyling not only for street wear, but under all professional conditions for all types of modeling assignments.

What you need to know about makeup

A model is constantly experimenting with different looks, using makeup in creative ways, trying to find new and interesting concepts of viewing himself/herself, discovering how to achieve a more natural appearance or a more exotic, high fashion one. You must be aware of changes in the marketplace, in order to keep up with trends and adapt your look accordingly.

Most models are familiar with a host of products; different makeups giving different finishes – matte, semi-matte, or glossy, for instance. Certain types of makeup may work in one situation but not in another – for example, panstick and pancake makeup are usually too heavy for street wear, but can be ideal under bright studio lighting, particularly for television cameras. Panstick and pancake have more staying power than natural, sheer types of makeup. For color photography, you will look for a softer, more natural foundation.

Street makeup is more subtle than that used for the camera, but even with a natural look, it is possible to minimize flaws and enhance assets. By experimenting with different products, you can learn what type coverage these products provide, how your skin reacts to them, what enhances you best, and how different makeup shades work with different color garments.

In order to photograph well, most models' skin needs the coverage makeup affords to smooth it out. A good base helps give an even coloration. The camera can add shine, lights may melt makeup, so you need frequent blotting, touching up and powdering. If a makeup artist is on set he takes care of this for you. If you are your own makeup artist, you'll have to monitor yourself. Usually photographers tell a model if his/her makeup needs repairing.

Makeup for go sees:

On go sees, callbacks and auditions, you should always look the part, to show the client you have the necessary requirements for the job. Often, this can be accomplished by varying makeup, wardrobe and hairstyle.

Be aware of different makeup styles suitable for different situations – for instance, on a go see to a conservative company or for an interview where you are called to be a middle American type, you would want to go in natural, unglamorous makeup.

Makeup for bookings

Find out in advance of a booking if there will be a makeup artist. If not, be prepared to check in with your makeup already done. You may wish to arrive in only light makeup, since you may have to adapt or change it in the course of the shoot – different effects may be required that you will add, layer by layer.

Neck and hands must match facial makeup, and sometimes, when modeling swimwear and lingerie, body makeup may be necessary as well. However, in such situations, usually a makeup artist is employed.

Creative experimenting

Models constantly experiment with their appearance. They watch how the pros apply makeup, what they use and why. When you work with makeup artists, ask their reasons for doing certain things, what effect they are striving for and why. Makeup artists are up on trends in looks and lighting, and can help models understand how to enhance their features for the camera. Study magazines, read articles on beauty and makeup. Try creating different looks on yourself.

Department stores offer makeovers at their cosmetics counters. Usually you are expected make a purchase, but since a model is always buying makeup of one sort or another anyway, this shouldn't be a problem. In your search for the best look, by letting knowledgeable people experiment on your face, you can always learn something new.

Most women start as teenagers learning about and experimenting with makeup, and continue the pursuit throughout their twenties, thirties and later. Watching home shopping channels - HSN, QVC, Shop NBC and others, as well as looking at YouTube videos for ideas will help hone your knowledge even more.

Makeup supplies a model needs

Foundation, concealer, contour and highlighting makeup, powder, eyeshadow and eyebrow brushes, eyeliner, mascara, cheek blush and brushes, lipsticks, lip brush and pencil, foam wedges, pencil sharpener are all tools the female model should own.

Each of the above products come in different shades and consistencies, provide different coverage and looks, and serve different purposes. A model should have an ample supply of the various types.

Beauty makeovers – Contouring and Highlighting – Corrective Makeup

Makeup can correct imperfections and enhance assets. Through highlighting and contouring, you can define, minimize or exaggerate bone structure and features, good and bad. Highlight makeup emphasizes, enlarges or brings out a feature, whereas contouring minimizes or conceals; contouring makeup is applied to those areas you want to recede, highlighting makeup to what you want emphasized. Even very plain girls can become extraordinary looking under the right conditions, given the right photographer, makeup and lighting.

Contouring and highlighting techniques can improve, correct, enhance, round, narrow, widen, flatten, broaden, lengthen, shorten, diminish, erase, or reshape facial features, and define planes for the camera's attention. If a forehead, nose or cheekbones are lightened, other features then recede.

If a face is wide and flat, lightening the center of the face will soften its contours. Using careful shading, you can enhance your strong features and cover for flaws. An overly square jaw or a face that would photograph too round, a face that's too thin, deep-set eyes – all of these can be exaggerated or minimized with the right makeup and lighting.

Experiment with different makeup, remembering to always blend foundation with concealer and highlighting and/or contour makeup as well as with blush and eyeshadow. Makeup should draw interest to your face, so always play up your best features, but be subtle about it.

Sometimes a feature you find unattractive in yourself someone else will view as distinctive and exciting, and that very feature could even make a career. How many people do you think told Lauren Hutton she should have corrective dentistry to fill in the gap in her teeth? When she was growing up, Cindy Crawford's sisters teased her about her mole, and later on, when Cindy was a fledgling model, one magazine even went so far as to airbrush it out of her photos. Male model Joel West was teased about his thick lips. Other people made all three of these models feel insecure about their appearance; yet all three were able to use the very features they were teased about as trademarks that set them apart from the pack.

Finishing touches - Be kind to your skin

– Cleanse, moisturize, and exfoliate skin

– Don't let problem skin get out of hand – see a dermatologist or cosmetician for repairs.

– Eat healthy foods, lots of fruits, vegetables, and whole grains; drink lots of water. Avoid too much salt, excess fats and sugars.

– If you get out in the sun, watch exposure. Wear a sunblock and a hat to protect yourself. Don't get too tan or you could lose jobs.

Makeup and hair for go sees

A model with experience, good skin and a good book may go out on auditions wearing a minimum of makeup if she is more comfortable that way. Some models prefer little to no makeup; others feel better with it. New models, however, are advised to put their best foot forward and feature an appearance that is neat and flattering.

Hair should be casual, well styled, in excellent shape, with a good cut (preferably a blunt cut, unless you have curly hair, which should also be properly styled and trimmed).

Hair care

A model needs hair that is both marketable and versatile. Keep hair trimmed to whatever length is the current look, groomed so that there are no messy split ends or stringiness. Hair must be in top condition, the more highlights and shine the better. Regular salon treatments are recommended.

Looking current is important. Some hairstyles seem never to go out of fashion, yet as with clothes and makeup, subtle differences appear year to year. Study magazines for inspiration. Be open to change if you are starting out, knowing that you must find a good look and maintain it for at least six months to a year as clients get to know you. At the same time, you should be adaptable, able to style your hair in different ways. Know how to create appropriate hairdos for a business look, a casual look, hairstyles appropriate for sportswear, high fashion, and glamour shots.

Your hair must have shape and texture. Make sure the style has no holes in it anywhere, particularly at the crown or sides. If you see gaps, fill them.

It's important to be able to create different and styles, but at the same time work within your type. If you are blond, don't suddenly go brunette or redhead without good reason and the sanction of your agency. Keep your look but know how to alter it. Clients can get confused if you are not true to type and if you don't resemble the pictures in your book and your composite.

A model's basic hairstyling supplies:

– Blow dryer
– Curling iron

– Hair accessories -- headbands, ribbons, combs, barrettes, etc.
– Natural bristle brushes (boar's head), wide tooth comb
– Shampoo, cream rinse, conditioner
– Heating cap for once a month deep conditioning
– Rollers in different sizes

When you are your own hairdresser

When a hairstylist is not in the budget, bring to a modeling job
your brushes, comb, blow dryer, hair spray and curling iron. The
latter three are necessary evils, detrimental to hair over long-term
use – but even so, they can be your salvation for quick fixes. If you
need a set, jiffy styling or repair, these tools are sometimes the
only answer.

Common sense haircare:

– Shampoo as often as hair needs to stay fresh and clean for
bookings and go sees
– Condition frequently
– Brush 100 times a day, head down
– Don't use elastic bands – they break the hair.
– Keep hair trimmed and conditioned.

Varieties of professional hair requirements

Sometimes you will be instructed to arrive in rollers or with your
hair already combed out. Other times, the stylist will shampoo and
set your hair on the job. In this case, you will usually have a very
early call, earlier than others on the booking.

Predetermine

Find out ahead of time what type assignment you are doing, what
is the concept, if there will be a stylist for the booking. Ask what

type of hairstyles are needed and any other client instructions. You also want to know the time element involved. If this is catalog work, you should be prepared to vary the hairstyle with each garment change.

Adapting and repairing hairstyles

In the midst of a shoot, adding fullness to the crown is often necessary, as is helping along hair that has wilted, by renewing volume. Repairs can be achieved through a quick reset, by using a curling iron, backcombing, backbrushing or teasing, or using hairspray, mousse or gel – all of which are hard on the hair over the long term. Sometimes brushing with the head down followed by tossing helps, and in some cases hair pieces may also do the trick.

Occasionally models are called upon to provide more extreme styles. You should be able to make various adjustments and be ready with new hairstyles such as crimping, kinks, spikes, wisps, more and less volume as called for; you should know how to work with different partings and sectionings, styles such as cornrows, chignons, French twists, pigtails, top knots, bangs and braids. You should get the knack of making your hair obey – curve it up and under, slick it back, accessorize it, work it with headbands, ribbons, bows, and floral decorations. You should also know how to work with wigs and other hairpieces, and it wouldn't hurt to own a few of these yourself.

Hair color

There are no hard and fast rules on color, and all shades are used, but very dark haired models must determine if their hair has sufficient highlights. If not, the hair could photograph like one big muddy blob, a photographic disaster. Black haired and dark brunettes may have to consider going lighter or at least adding highlights.

CHAPTER 8 - WORKING WITH PHOTOGRAPHERS

Camera-ease

A good model puts herself in the photographer's hands and lets him direct a shoot. Never give a photographer instructions or try to clue him in on what you think are your photographic strong suits. Each photographer sees differently, and it's his job to shoot, not yours; his is the vision that matters, not yours. Even so, you as the model can sometimes make a contribution in the realm of creative ideas, as with experience and seasoning, your intuition develops.

Eventually, a model will gain ease in front of the camera, and become in tune with the natural rhythm of a shoot. Novices often appear nervous and afraid, which is why they don't come across as well in photos as the pros. Beginners who lack confidence seem confused or distracted, get into wrong positions, assume poor facial expressions, which is why they need seasoning to bring out the best in them.

What can you do to make things easier for the photographer, and be more adaptive in a shoot?

– Become more light-sensitive; pick up an understanding of light and lighting.

– Ask the photographer why he made his choices

– Examine critically your movements, gestures, expressions, and features that either stand out favorably or don't work. Ask yourself why one expression is uninteresting or another works well.

– Keep a record of all tests and review them several times.

– Work on relating better to the camera.

– For a more relaxed eye expression, look away without focusing, then look back; find a point off camera to gaze at, then return your eyes to the camera or at a point where the photographer asks you to focus on.

Stay alert to the photographer's mood, taking your cues intuitively. Ideally, energy should flow naturally between model and photographer. Others on set often feel it and can tell when a shoot was successful.

Different conditions

With practice, you will come to know the difference between working with color, black and white, various speeds and types of film, types of lighting, and what makeup is best for each. Most photographers, editors, cameramen, and studio makeup artists want to be helpful and will be pleased to advise beginners by giving directions and offering the benefit of their knowledge.

– Try to see how you look under the lights. Ask the makeup artist to hold up a mirror for you under the lights; or you may see yourself on the monitor.

– Sometimes the cameraman or photographer will let you look through the lens when the shot is set up. Someone else on set may cooperate by standing in your position so you can get a better idea of the setup.

– Know what type of shot you are in and see if there is anything you can do to improve your appearance for it. Know if you are shooting a closeup, extreme tight closeup, or longshot. When possible, ask questions.

– Learn about lighting, angles and lenses, so you are aware of the technical aspects of photography. Is the photographer using a wide angle, zoom or telephoto lens, a 180 portrait lens?

– Outdoor light, also called available light, changes throughout the day. Best times to photograph are mornings before noon and at the end of the day, after 4 p.m. Overcast days are also good. As the model, you may not have a choice, but you should be aware of these things, nonetheless.

– Be aware of lighting, its quality, direction, and color; types of lighting, such as single source and multiple source, sunlight, available light at different times of day, studio lighting, umbrellas, foil and reflectors, strobe, kleigs, lekes, tungsten, fluorescent lighting, and so forth.

– Light direction may come from above or below, from the side, from behind, or all of the above. Aiming the face in the direction of the light is usually best for photographic shoots.

– Available light in spring is different than in fall, different on the east coast than the west, different in Florida, California – different in Italy than Germany, the Caribbean, Hawaii.

– The light of a sunset is warm, making the skin look warmer. Harsh lighting is cooler. Are you being photographed in flat lighting? Soft, diffused lighting? High voltage studio lights can conceal blemishes, but may cause perspiration and necessitate frequent blotting.

– The sun brings oils to the skin's surface, but may be attractive to a male model's overall skin texture.

You may have to make subtle makeup changes based on lighting angles, degree and intensity. For instance, you may need a heavier base or a lighter, more natural, water-based foundation that is nearly imperceptible. You may need to accentuate the eyes, use more blush. Lighting is very important and can be used to create different moods, to actually alter a model's appearance or enhance it.

Lighting sometimes makes a model uncomfortable. The model has to learn to keep the eyes open, not to squint. One trick is to close your eyes, then open them just before the shot.

Other technical aspects

The photographer may be using wind machines, fans, motor drives, dolley shots, or other variations that you will encounter in assignments over and over again.

Posing

The very term "posing" suggests something static and unnatural, whereas the key in modeling is to be relaxed and fluid in front of a camera. Some say ease before the lens is something a model either has intuitively or picks up in time, while in the process of working.

Some photographers give pointers on the job; others expect the model to already know what's expected. Some photographers explain what they want to the model by assuming a pose themselves; some give elaborate directions, while others leave it up to the model to improvise. Models eventually learn to discern the subtle signals and body language involved with working with a photographer.

Every photographer has a different style; some photographers talk, others are silent, some joke, some play their favorite music, which can vary from Bach to the Beatles to the Beastie Boys, or Arcade Fire to Aida.

Changing positions

Changing position in front of the camera is usually subtle – sudden changes are seldom made, particularly in catalog work. Avoid any shift in position that is too bold or broad, unless instructed otherwise by the photographer. A model's head movements should be small. Don't jerk; move covering a small area at a time. Facial movements should be kept minimal, nearly imperceptible, body movements aligned with the photographer's instructions. Sometimes movement will be restricted and other times the model has more freedom. Take your cues form the photographer, including what to do with your arms and hands.

The photographer lets you know when he's gotten a shot. His assistants draw his attention to any detail that would spoil the shot (label showing, jacket buttoned wrong). The photographer tells the model which angles work best relative to the lighting, whether to tilt a head or lower it to eliminate puffs and bags, watch clothing creases and bunching, look up, look down, tilt, turn, raise your head, slow motion clockwise and counterclockwise, change your thoughts, react to things in the room, around you or internally.

The photographer may tell you how he wants you to position your chin, to look at a certain spot, to be as if engaged in an activity, glance a certain way or reflect a particular mood. Your eyes have to be varied, expressions contact-full. Raise or lower your focus, readjust, and keep it fresh. Elongate the neck. Stand, sit, kneel, and lie down, as you and the photographer get deeper into it. As you change the placement of your hands, position them on your body; move them to your face, hair, to the garment, and put them in your pockets.

Vary your feet position, stance, and spread, point your toes, vary weight placement. Move in rhythm. Try arching your back, stretching, twisting, holding your breath and sucking it in, keeping other muscles taut, then relaxed; try a forward thrust and an elongation of the torso.

Frequently a model's movements are directed by the photographer in signals that no one but the photographer and model are aware of, as the two synch their harmony together. Feel as though there is an invisible cord connecting you and the photographer. A photographer often send out subtle signals to the model what he wants: he moves his shoulders, arms or hips and the model unconsciously imitates by following his lead.

Keep in mind:

– You always want to appear taller, straighter, and more graceful. Never slouch. Always keep a tall line when you sit, and keep your head up.

– Observe other models and copy the best of the best. To get an idea of a model's basic stances, study fashion magazines, catalogs, DVD's, YouTube and videos. Observe the different positions a model assumes standing: how do the hands move? Where are they placed – at the sides, folded in front, fingers interlocked, arms crossed, hands on hips, on thighs, touching face or hair, hands in pockets? Study different options – you should eventually use them all yourself.

– Walk with head up, heels down, weight centered. Step lightly, and feel a diamond shape in your diaphragm when you move. Let the arms swing slightly.

– Sitting: lower yourself into a chair gracefully; rise gracefully as well. Sit at an angle. Cross legs at knees or at ankles.

– Keep your back straight when in repose; when working, vary your position with arched, curved or twisted back, leaning your body.

– Lean against the wall, sit on a stool, raise a shoulder, sit sideways on a chair, lean forward or backwards.

– Do away with distracting mannerisms.

Sometimes in modeling you will assume postures and positions that wouldn't look good in real life, poses that are stylized or exaggerated, but which work perfectly for the camera and serve to create a mood. Make the clothes look like they're meant for you by capitalizing on your best points. Make everything look easy and have fun with it. Watch and copy other models, learn from pictures and videos, practice moving with fluidity and grace. Surf the net and study what you come across. There is so much material available of models working all over the world in different capacities, both in photos and videos, that you can pick up pointers galore via that method.

When things aren't working

A smile gets dull and frozen fast. Models can overcome this mechanical problem by moving the head every time a picture is ready to be snapped, then settling into the shot at the last second. Puff out your cheeks, close your eyes, look away, then return your gaze and make sure the expression is alive at the very last split second.

On Being Photogenic

You don't have to be beautiful to be photogenic, but you do have to have something arresting that the camera captures. What is photogenic? It's a quality that can be projected at any age, by any and all category of model. Being photogenic is conveying your unique and arresting quality with immediacy and impact. Look at other models' photos. Are they exceptionally gorgeous? Many are not, yet are special and project something extraordinary. If you study old pictures of today's famous models, you will see the difference in how they looked at the outset of their careers. In fact, you may wonder what anyone ever saw in them in the first place!

Modeling tips:

– Treat the camera as your best friend, or your lover.

– Study yourself in the mirror, assume different attitudes and poses. Think various thoughts and see what your reactions are.

– Take a piece of paper, cut out a circle the size of a camera lens. Tape it to a mirror, stand 6 feet away, talk directly to the hole to practice reading for commercials.

– Work, live, and travel among the fashionable, Exposing yourself to taste and culture develops a keener eye and deeper appreciation of fashion's creative side. Keep it fresh.

Second nature bring alongs

Always bring a voucher, and get it signed

Bring your tote or carryall, full of your modeling bling and goodies. On daily travels to and from assignments and interviews, bring everything you may need for a booking, interview or emergency – in your model's tote, be sure you have all the makeup and hair care supplies you might need. Extra pantyhose, undergarments, and accessories all belong in your tote. Some days you may need other tools of the trade – blow dryer, curling iron, rollers, plus extra shoes, glasses, hats, and hair ornaments.

CHAPTER 9 - MARKETS - USA

It bears repeating that the primary model markets are New York, London, Paris, Milan, and Tokyo. Secondary US markets are Los Angeles, Chicago, and Miami. Atlanta, Boston, Philadelphia, Texas (Dallas/Houston), Las Vegas, and Seattle are strong regional markets as well.

Secondary foreign markets are Zurich, Munich, Hamburg, Denmark, Sweden, Barcelona, Madrid, Rome, Florence, Mexico City, Australia, Canada (Toronto, Montreal, etc.).

Other good regional US markets: Arizona, the Carolinas, New Orleans, Cleveland, Detroit, Tampa, Orlando, Hawaii.

Local modeling: markets

Starting out, a model needs experience and exposure. One of the best ways to become bookable in the larger markets is to first model in the secondary ones. These exist in every city of the country. If you already live in or near one of them, you would be wise to seek out an agency close to home.

When a New York-based account is traveling to another area to do a promotion, they may hire locally to save on the higher cost of New York models. Additionally, regional markets are active modeling centers in themselves. These secondary markets are plugged into the international markets, and a good agent from cities small and large can feed a model into other markets, whether New York, Paris, Milan, London, Germany, Japan or wherever. Today, a good model can tap into any market he or she chooses and be booked anywhere in the world. But the model must have some background to be able to get immediate bookings in a major city.

Smaller markets are good places to work in the early stages of a model's career; the pace is slower and the cost of living lower, as a rule. Regional markets offer everything – print, high fashion, runway, showroom, television. The only possible danger in small markets is overexposure, but your agency can alert you if this is happening, when it's time to move on to another market to expand your horizons.

Regional, secondary market agencies will sign models and become that model's "home agency" or "mother agency." Development is an agency's function. When ready, a model from a smaller market is fed into a larger one.

Almost every city has an active modeling market. Some specialize, like Detroit, where most of the work is connected to the auto industry. Seattle is a popular stop-off for agents and photographers from France, Italy, Germany and Japan, who scout there twice a year. Arizona, with its warm climate and interesting backgrounds, has a thriving modeling industry.

Atlanta is a good place to initiate a modeling career. Out of towners who come here can do well. Atlanta is an active market with lots of catalog and convention work and has one of the largest apparel marts in the country, offering wholesale models plenty of work.

Florida is the third largest film and television market in the country. Models, magazines and film crews flock to Miami from all over the world, both for the weather, the backgrounds and Florida mystique. Florida is a state that's easy to get around in; from Miami, it's a few hours' drive to Tampa or Orlando, both modeling and film centers. There is less competition in Miami than in New York, Los Angeles or the European markets. If you have what it takes, you should be kept busy in Miami.

Pros in some smaller markets

Another southern city, albeit smaller, is Wilmington, North Carolina, the home of Delia Model Management. Delia heads an active development and model management company. On display in her office, Delia posts magazine covers on which her models have appeared – Italian Vogue, Marie-Claire, American Health, New Woman, Elle, Seventeen, Glamour, Mademoiselle and a host of others. Her girls have been featured in many other prestigious international publications as well.

Says Delia, "I work with major agencies in New York and around the world, all out of little Wilmington, North Carolina, and I know that Ford recommends me, as well as Paris/USA and several others. I serve as Mother Agent very well, and being down here in this day of computers and faxes helps me stay on top of everything."

Yet another busy North Carolina agency is Directions, USA. Directions handles photographic models with excellent portfolios, books models for print, runway and commercials.

Many Boston accounts include hi tech and audio visual companies in such mediums as commercial, print and live modeling. Boston offers lots of work to infants and children, and adult models can be booked from the 20's to 50's, especially if they look like business types for executive training brochures and sales training manuals.

Model Club Kids, Boston, represents children throughout the United States, provides both print and television work. The agency's model earnings range from between $50,000 to $100,000 a year.

Darrel Rawlins of First Model Management Inc., Honolulu, handles men, women, and children, models and talent of all ages over four years old, and the agency has some of the top people in the Hawaiian market. They are full service in all markets – local, national, and international. Darrel's advice to aspiring models: "Be a good listener, stay focused, develop your style and practice every second. You have to be hungry to make it."

Favra Bickerton, who runs Bickerton Models in Toronto, says: "Our top models have appeared in Italian Elle, Marie-Claire, Details, Paris Show, and in major campaigns for Eaton's, Canada's top department store." Bickerton provides work in commercials, print, runway, and international model placement. Favra's suggestions and advice to hopeful models: "Study fashion magazines to see if you can really see yourself and identify with the models in those magazines. A model must not only focus on marketing herself as a beautiful woman, but someone with a high level of professionalism, energy, enthusiasm and a strong sense of confidence!"

Bickerton also runs a children's division, Applause Model Management. "Our kids have appeared in numerous mall fashion shows, magazines," says Favra.

Also Toronto-based, with branches in Ottawa and Montreal, is Angie's Models & Images Talent, which handles fashion, commercials, kids, men and character types, and does print and runway advertising as well. Advice from Angies's: "Keep up with your training and development. Test, test, test with the best photographers. Attend the IMTA convention (q.v.) in New York or Los Angeles."

Dallas and Houston books dozens of models daily for shoots, live fashion shows and other store promotions. Casting for catalog and other print media occurs on a regular basis, and many European photographers and magazines who come to Texas to shoot hire local models. Models who would be considered over the hill in other markets can have a renewed career in Texas, especially those models with previous market week experience. Local agencies usually send models to Europe for further training prior to sending them to New York.

Page Parkes is the largest model and talent agency in the Southwest; headquartered in Houston, with branches in Dallas and Miami. The Page Parkes Corporation umbrellas the InterMedia Model & Talent Agency, Page Parkes Center of Modeling, Page Parkes Model's Rep, Page Parkes & Michael's Hair Salon, Model Camp, InterMedia and the Center of Modeling.

A former model herself, Page Parkes opened her agency doors in

1981. Her InterMedia (Houston) represents over 400 models for print, runway and commercials; Page Parkes Model's Rep in Dallas, which opened in '85, has launched many of the world's most famous faces; Page Parkes' Miami Model's Rep opened in 1989; (the Florida market is second only to New York in demand for models, says Page Parkes).

Asked, "How does a model know if he/she has what it takes?" Page Parkes replies, "Ask a professional agency – or more than one; ask several." As a general guideline, however, fashion and runway models "should be at least 5'8, have a well proportioned figure with long, shapely legs. Males should be between 5'11 and 6'2, with a medium athletic build. There is no set look in facial features. Good teeth, healthy skin and hair are standard requirements." Shorter female models can do petite runway and petite fashion print; short male and female models – if they are outgoing, expressive, and animated, can do commercial print and acting.

"Commercial print is where a talent sells a product or service in the form of print media, demonstrating the ability to clearly communicate attitudes and emotions nonverbally – done through facial expressions and body language; wardrobe is incidental, used more or less as a prop to support the situation. Commercial print models are regularly seen in national billboards, magazines, newspapers, in television commercials, industrials, and movies. There are no age or height requirements, and the work can be done throughout one's entire life. The financial rewards are excellent."

Be sure your book is appropriate for the market you are aiming for, says Page. "You need the opinion of an agency in the market to which you aspire. The agency can tell if your portfolio is competitive enough to generate client interest, and the agency can also show you how to build a more competitive book – using makeup artists, stylists, and photographers." Page adds that most professionals who excel live in larger markets; smaller towns don't usually offer a wide range of top talent in these fields.

Chicago is a product and advertising city, a city with a huge convention center, a large merchandise mart, a thriving television commercial industry, and many other advantages for models. Convention models can make excellent money in Chicago, and catalog models can earn $1000 a day and more on an almost daily basis.

If a model comes to Chicago with a good composite and portfolio, she can work almost immediately. As in Texas, girls who don't find jobs in larger markets like New York, Europe and Japan can often make great money in Chicago. Here, a model doesn't have to be as tall as in other markets; she can be as short as 5'5 – what counts in Chicago is the face.

Los Angeles loves its pretty women, but can be a tough market, due to competition from the city's unending supply of incredibly beautiful women. To succeed here, a model should be young, fresh-faced, ambitious and hard working. As a rule, Los Angeles calls for a different style of model than other markets, the image being oriented toward glamour and movie star sex appeal. A lot of work is available for bathing suit, lingerie and nude models. Downtown Los Angeles has a merchandise mart and a garment center, where California sportswear is a popular category requiring models.

The emphasis in L.A. is on film, and it is unusual for a talent to specialize solely in modeling; most models are aspiring actors and actresses who accept work in all mediums. Many models find it's not difficult for models to mix with Hollywood stars socially, and to meet industry insiders. Even so, competition remains a big factor.

New York – The Apex

New York is the world capital of modeling, the pinnacle of professionalism, the city where modeling is most a business. New York is for pros. For a New York career, a fashion model needs tear sheets, published pictures of her work in magazines and newspapers. However, these are difficult to obtain in New York;

the field is competitive, crowded, and rough for beginners. Consequently, most New York-based models have trained elsewhere.

"Everyone is international today," says David Bosman, Boss New York. All top New York agencies have branch offices or affiliates everywhere in the world. Modeling in the US has become a national network with an international arm that permits models to move anywhere on the globe. Small and medium sized markets feed models into larger ones. To be ready for New York, in all but the luckiest and most unusual situations, (a model with the right connections), the model has to have done groundwork elsewhere – preferably abroad.

Models who lean more toward the television and talent end of the business might be advised to come to New York even without background and experience, in order to study with New York's acting teachers, generally known to be the best in the country, and to take other classes. However, models without an interest in theatre and film should make sure they have some regional modeling experience before tackling New York.

Jeffrey Kolsrud of Q Model Management's advice to aspiring models: "Be persistent, trust your agents. Find one person or agency you are comfortable with and listen to them, not to everyone that wants to give you advice."

The Lyons Group, Lights, Camera, Flex, handles sports, athletic, fitness, catalog, and commercial print. Their advice: "Find the right agent/manager, don't pay an agency to work with you. Shop several agencies before making a decision."

CHAPTER 10 - INTERNATIONAL MARKETS

New York as well as regional agencies ("home agencies" or "mother agencies") send models to Europe and monitor their performance; the model returns with a great book and tear sheets; progress then goes faster because the model has worked with top photographers, and clients see they have an impressive European background. Once a model has Milan or Paris exposure, he/she gets all kinds of bookings on the other side of the Atlantic.

Europe is an integral part of a fashion model's career for many reasons: most countries have more prestigious fashion publications than the US has; thus, the European market can offer a greater opportunity to launch a career. Building your portfolio in Europe adds polish and clients to your credentials. Attitudes are more relaxed in Europe, a good fashion sense can be acquired quickly, while Europe molds the model in positive directions that will attract Stateside clients. The fresh, unsophisticated American girl who lacks the mystery and je ne sais quoi of a European mannequin can pick up pointers and polish in Europe that will command attention back home.

There is something compelling about the continental atmosphere – Europe's lighting, backgrounds, sites, aura. Added to that, a wide variety of different venues are available in close proximity to each other. Modeling wages in Europe may be lower than in the US, but the model's investment in his future is well worth it.

European layouts are more artistic than American ones, photographers more innovative than their American counterparts, probably because they are allowed greater creative freedom. International tear sheets with a continental flavor are an important adjunct to a model's career. Moreover, US magazines are not as well printed as Europe's.

In Europe, models are not expected to be perfect. Slight flaws that would never be acceptable in US markets are considered interesting in Europe. A European experience gives the fledgling model elegance and worldliness, making him/her more professional and more sought after at home.

After returning to the States, models continue working with European photographers, magazines and designers by being booked around the world, keeping two careers going. They do collections, editorial, beauty, and fly back and forth countless times a year. Many accounts are regulars that call for the same models over and over again.

Europe, comprised of so many active cities offering so much work, has hundreds of magazine outlets for modeling talent. Milan leads the pack, with more fashion magazines than any other city in the world; Paris and London follow suit. Milan is very editorial; Germany is mainly catalog. It's great prestige to model all over the continent. Being in Europe, one is centrally positioned, at the epicenter of the booming international scene. European agencies work closely with a model to find a look, groom her/him to suit their particular market, and land assignments that enhance the model's career on both sides of the Atlantic.

International modeling is more laid back, except in Japan, where workaholic Japanese clients may book models on assignments continuing for as long as 16 straight hours and more without pause. In Paris and Milan shoots, people take time out to enjoy a long lunch, nor is a model penalized for being late to assignments – indeed, in those markets showing up late is an occupational hazard. The German fashion capitals of Hamburg and Munich as well as London adhere to professional rules closer to those in the US, however.

Heights aren't as rigid in some cities abroad. In Japan, a 5'6" model who couldn't work in New York can work in Tokyo and Osaka. Some markets can help you overcome an impediment that might have held you back in New York, so that when you return it's no longer a problem – your tear sheets and experience compensate, making you a more marketable commodity in the US.

One finds all types of agencies throughout Europe and Japan, everything from small boutique agencies to completely computerized large ones with large staffs specializing in editorial, runway and TV, with strong men's and children's divisions.

Many agencies are selective when it comes to accepting overseas models, since not all foreigners will fit in with the lifestyle in other countries. Some models are too young and irresponsible to be on their own in a foreign country; they are not internationally savvy, lack polish and social skills. It takes a pioneering nature and confidence to move around the continent, particularly if you are unfamiliar with the territory and speak no foreign languages. For someone who has never been abroad before, Europe or Japan are apt to present a culture shock.

A model can face a host of new challenges abroad. On a daily basis, you will be confronted with predicaments: languages, money, customs, surface travel, shopping, food, unfamiliar surroundings – everything can require an adjustment. You may be climbing thousands of wide, hard to mount cement or marble stairs in buildings with no elevators (or riding creaky, old ones), working in old, cold, drafty castles, even using disgusting toilet facilities that are a mere step above outhouses.

You will have to adapt to the metric system of weights and measures, using centimeters, meters and kilometers instead of inches, feet and miles, and kilos instead of pounds, or the British system of stones; a different system of weather, (Centigrade rather than Fahrenheit), the confusing 24 hour clock, foreign clothing sizes (British and Continental) and European shoe sizes can be added dilemmas. In some cases, Europe may lack comforts Americans take for granted; the bathroom (which may be known as the W.C., *toilette, cabinet, gabinetto*, lavatory, ladies, *Herren, Damen* or other strange to Anglo ears' name) may be a facility down the hall shared with several other people, and the toilet paper may be disappointing by American standards – stiff in texture, shiny and dirty beige in appearance. Hot water may be rationed and difficult to come by. Adapting to new customs such as these can be daunting. Sometimes a model does not react well to the city chosen, or may have communication problems.

Agents work together as an international network, feeding models back and forth to each other. An international model's comp card will list affiliates: "London, Paris, Copenhagen, Toronto, Taiwan, Milan, Mexico City, Sidney, Japan, Los Angeles, New York," and so forth, with the name of the agency in each location. It is certainly best to go to Europe with the backing and blessing of a home agency. Ideally, you should send photos ahead to work up interest, and arrive with an agency expecting you.

This is not to say going to Europe cold can't be done: it can and has been, but usually those who fare best in this scenario are those who speak at least one foreign language, have previously traveled internationally, and find it easy to deal with new situations.

Americans sometimes have a difficult time abroad, because so many have led narrow lives; they come from small town environments, and are unaccustomed to European sophistication, whereas Europeans have been dealing with people from many different cultures all their lives. Europeans adapt easily, as they are raised to be polyglots and are familiar with the cultures of their neighboring countries.

For those planning to model abroad, it wouldn't hurt to buy a language tape (or a few) before you leave, although nothing equals total immersion, requiring learning on the spot. Still, a tape can pre-accustom and condition. Once you arrive, start buying the country's newspapers and magazines, watch their television, and begin assimilating the local habits. Before long, you will begin to be conversant, and in six months, you'll be amazed how far you've come with another language, if you really make the effort. But resist the urge to speak English! If those who book you insist on using English with you, then be polite and oblige, but find other outlets in your non-working hours.

Read as much as possible before going, talk to other models, and try to get answers to your questions prior to leaving home. If you are near a major US city, you might drop in on the country's

Consulate General or visit their travel center to collect information.

Europe is more expensive than the US, and Japan is even more so. Many models arrive in a foreign country with insufficient funds and may experience homesickness; some are too young to be sent abroad without supervision but go anyway, which is a mistake. To go to Europe, a model must be well adjusted, self-reliant, and resourceful.

Most foreign countries are not as organized as we are, even on the regional level. They move at a slower pace, and definitely less professional. Germany is the major exception, the Germans being known for their organization and efficiency. In general, Switzerland and Germany are considered the safest European countries. Most American models will, if given the chance, prefer working in Paris, Milan or London, the latter due to the comfort of dealing with a population that speaks the same language, the former two because of the savoir-faire, charm and sophistication of the people.

Being in Europe as a model can mean traveling all over, and it can also mean being invited to elegant parties, to weekends in beautiful homes and cruises on fabulous yachts. A model with these options has to balance distractions with career.

Before a model leaves for abroad, the Stateside agent gives a list of clients to see, to be compared with the list to be given by the agency upon arrival in Europe. Americans should come to Europe prepared with the proper clothing, makeup and accessories, the latter which should always be brought to assignments. Since accessories are not a requisite in the US, American girls may be unprepared and not own a proper set, while Europeans, on the other hand, are frequently booked partly based on the quality of their accessories wardrobe.

Be aware that in Eurozone nations, you will have to pay a VAT (value added) tax on your purchases, which raises the cost of goods.

Germany

Germany is a good place to start on the international modeling scene, because it offers a tremendous amount of catalog work. Foreign models are in demand here; scores of Americans are currently living and working in both Hamburg and Munich.

While this is not the country for tear sheets, most German pictures being unacceptable for models' portfolios in New York, Paris, London and Milan, what Germany does offer is experience and the chance to earn money. The market has a good deal of editorial work, but since the German look is different, their tear sheets are unsuitable for other markets. The benefit is that due to the prevalence of catalog work in Germany, you can be kept busy, save money and prepare for other markets.

Germany operates on rules; in this respect, it is the antithesis of Italy. Many agencies will hand a model a complete book of rules and regulations; it is up to you to familiarize yourself with them and obey them. If a girl arrives with a good book she can work within days, otherwise, it will take her a minimum of two weeks, maybe even up to six to nine months or longer to work, depending upon circumstances.

Behind every agency is a finance company, insuring that you will be paid on time. If an agent takes you on, you are automatically granted work permission and there is no tax on earnings. You work for a fee, pay a commission to the finance company, and keep the rest. Agencies pay promptly, sometimes the same day as the job.

Hamburg is a big market with lots of magazines and catalogs. The city is friendly, civilized, sophisticated, worldly yet conservative, most residents speak English, and there are many superlative restaurants; in fact, one of the world's top ten, Landhaus Scherrer, is located in Hamburg. (Be forewarned that lunch for two here can run several hundred dollars).

Local agents scout and recruit internationally, and once an agency takes a model on, they devote a great deal of time teaching the ropes, outlining agency policy, planning the future. They phone photographers and hairdressers, round up clothes and set up tests. They will also find a model living accommodations, perhaps with another model.

When someone new arrives, the agency will meet with her, take measurements, look over her pictures and book, review agency policy, assist in transportation and other information, and immediately arrange for tests and go-sees. Prior to starting out on a go see, models must check in at the agency in person at 10 am.

A full day booking is 9 hours, including lunch; a half day is four hours. On overtime, the first half hour is free, every hour thereafter is chargeable. Your agency booker must be informed within 24 hours of overtime to be negotiated. Cancellations must be made at least 5 days prior to a shoot on multi-day bookings, or for a single day booking, 36 hours prior.

Any model failing to show up for a booking is liable for the day's full production cost, including other models' fees; not showing for a location shooting also includes liability for flight, travel, hotel costs, and all other fees incurred by the client, photographer, stylist, other models, and everyone connected with the shoot. A model will be sued in his country of residence or the costs will be deducted from his agency account.

On trips outside Germany, the client pays hotel and meals; within Germany, the client pays taxis, hotel and breakfast only. Expenses will be paid only if bills are received by the agency within 5 days of booking completion.

Hamburg Airport (Flughafen Hamburg-Fuhlsbüttel) lies about five miles from the center of the city and is linked to the city by both bus and subway. The bus stop is to the left of the exit doors, at the airport's lower level. An airport express bus leaves every 10 minutes for Ohlsdorf station, serviced by the U-Bahn (subway) train. Tickets can be purchased on a daily basis, or you may obtain a weekly or monthly card that requires a photo, which you can buy at the central station (the Hauptbahnhof). The station also has automatic ticket machines. Do not hail a taxi from the side of the road but wait for one at a taxi stand.

Hamburg has an exciting culture, great theatre and shopping, more bridges than Venice or Amsterdam, and more fountains than Rome. It's a noted seaport and apt to get chilly in early fall. Bring warm clothing if you plan to be in the city in November and thereafter.

Munich, considered the fashion capital of Germany, is known for its Oktoberfest, (annual beer drinking festival), and for Fasching, a carnival that lasts from Epiphany to Mardi Gras. March and October are Modewochen – Fashion Weeks – in Munich. Life here is less formal than in Hamburg, but modeling standards are stiffer; clients want experienced models, and expect value for their money. Beginners are not encouraged. Before you will be seen by a client, the client asks to see your comp card (Sed card).

As in Hamburg, each model upon arrival at the agency receives a booklet explaining the agency's rules and regulations. The agency will also give out the names, addresses and phone numbers of photographers, magazines, and ad agencies they want you to see. Typical of the well-organized German manner, under each name is written transportation information, directing you to bus or subway (U-Bahn, S-Bahn, etc).

Initial weeks are spent testing and seeing clients. It takes time to get the right composite for Munich and to start working. If after three weeks no jobs have been offered and there is no interest on the part of clients, the model is re-assessed, and may be sent elsewhere.

It's easy for American men to work in Munich and their look is popular. All kinds of looks are requested, and men can work past the age of 50.

Paris

Paris is so chic, so exciting and romantic. There is something about it, a certain je *ne sais quoi* that is infectious and exhilarating, which you sense even as you arrive at either Charles de Gaulle Airport or at Orly. Models come to Paris to model during Christmas, Easter and summer vacations, and many decide to become based there. It takes time to get Paris tear sheets, although France has any number of fashion magazines. Still, it's a highly competitive market, with many agencies vying for a piece of the pie.

French women have a knack for turning themselves out and are recognized as having an instinctive fashion sense. Even a woman who is not a great beauty can look fabulous because she finds just the right touch that makes an outfit and thus her overall presentation. *Elle a du chien* is a phrase often used to describe French women; Americans face formidable competition in Paris not only from French models but from those from all over the world. Nevertheless, traditionally, over many decades, American models have always been popular in France.

Models flock to Paris from everywhere for the celebrated haute couture collections in January and July, and again for *the prêt à porter* (ready to wear) in March, September and October. In August, model agencies are closed and Paris itself is nearly deserted, its population enjoying a well-deserved *congé* (holiday).

A few things you need to know if you are planning to work in Paris:

– An organization called Le Syndicat des Agences de Mannequin (SAM) gives models guidelines on rates, rules and regulations, and defines laws on royalties, TV and poster rates.

– Documents are required to live and work in France. You must keep these up to date.

– *Sécurité sociale* means government reimbursement for medical expenses. As a resident of France, you will be eligible.

A staff member at your French agency will take care of your working papers. Accompany the staff member to the police station; sign required papers, submit 8 passport size photos to apply for a social security number, work permit and six months *carte de séjour* (residence permit).

A few weeks later you will be required to take a medical exam. Return to the police station to pick up your residence permit. You may renew this twice and it must never expire. If you change agencies, documents are invalid and you have to start all over again with the new agency. You must observe all rules, or the agency will be prosecuted and you will be deported.

You need three portfolios for work in Paris, your own, one for the agency to keep, and one to be sent around Paris to clients who want to pre-select models from their books before the first interview.

Although height requirements are the usual 5'9 to 11, there are exceptions. The maximum hip measure for the collections is 34". A pleasant attitude, energy, posture and professionalism are important in Paris. Male models need good pictures and tear sheets to work. Some American men tend to look too California or beach boyish for Paris, but the elegant, worldly and mysterious type male is popular and can work till age 50, 60 and more, if he is still in shape.

The busy Paris market could be intimidating to the newcomer, as the level of competition is high, and some French models seem unfriendly, arrogant and clannish to outsiders. But if you are motivated and professional you will work.

Many of the leading Paris agencies have apartments for foreign models, as do some of the big New York agencies who work with them. Since Paris is expensive, you will want to have enough money available for at least three to six months, in case it takes you a while to start working. Also, you should know that Paris does not have the reputation of paying models with the same efficiency as Germany. Be prepared that you might have to wait for your checks.

You will probably want to travel on the efficient Paris Métro, the subway system. A book of 10 tickets is called a carnet. You can buy a monthly pass with your name, photo and signature, or you can buy the orange carte *hébdomadaire*, weekly card. However, the Métro can be threatening to the outsider who speaks no French. Study subway maps, and try to locate your destination ahead of time. If you look lost you're a target for underground robbers. Paris, like many cities, has its share of petty thieves scouting for vulnerable easy targets.

Gas station attendants, theatre and cinema attendants should be tipped in France. *Servis compris*, which appears on all restaurant tabs, means tip included. If change is returned with your payment of a bill, leave it behind for the waiter as well.

Au Printemps, the Galeries Lafayette, au Bon Marché, the rue du Faubourg St. Honoré, Avenue Montaigne, Rue Tronchet and the Champs-Elysées are great places to browse and shop. Paris has outstanding boutiques, and of course you will also want to visit the Louvre, the Left Bank, Pompidou Center, the famous Marché aux Puces (flea market), and Les Halles, where you can still get a great bowl of Paris' well known *soupe à l'oignon* (onion soup).

Milan

The world fashion scene starts in Milan (Milano to Italians), then switches to London, Paris and New York, in a collection season six weeks long that opens in October at Milan's Fiera Campionaria. Models come here from all over the world, and Milan, with more international magazines than any other city in the world, offers tons of work. There is tremendous competition here, although you don't need tear sheets to work – you can start with a handful of test shots. A model who trains in Milan can work anywhere. Inside of three months, you should have built a good book, and in six months you will have outstanding tear sheets.

Milan is a fabulous city, glamorous and exciting. Some agencies have apartments or can help models find an inexpensive *pensione* (full meal plan or half). Agencies will also arrange work permits.

What a model needs is the right look for the market, excellent hair and figure, stamina, drive and personality. Models who are the right type and come with a good book should work within 10 days. Otherwise, in some instances, it could take six months to get the right photos. Good models are usually kept busy 5 days a week.

It is estimated that 60% of models working in Milan are American. One thing Italians prize about American models is that they are very professional. Although rates are not high in Milan, it is an incomparable training ground. Versace, Missoni, Armani, Gucci, Fendi, and other famous names in alta moda (high fashion) and pronto a portare (ready to wear) make highly desirable clients.

Models invading Italy ideally should have a reputable home agent who knows the international scene and has good connections in Milan. In Milan, the agencies take 50% of a model's fee, and it's hard to figure out what you're really earning, even though they provide written statements. Also, checks may be inordinately delayed.

Milan is fabled for its nightclub and party scene, and for its notoriously charming and irresistible playboys. Superficially, Milan playboys may impress with their courtly manners. A European girl would see through them quicker than the American who lacks experience in dealing with European men.

A frank assessment from an admitted Italian playboy, a high profile marchese who prefers to remain anonymous: "The agents don't like their girls going out with these bad people, which in Italian we call *gente per male*, or *gentaccia*. But the models somehow gravitate to men *in gamba*, without understanding that they are just looking to cheat on their wives. The Italian male mentality is always to believe that their wives, their sisters and daughters would never give a man the horns. The Italian man takes a vulnerable young American girl to his *garconnière*, and at the same time, whether he likes it or not, ironically, he is most likely being *cornuto* (cuckolded) himself. My advice to American models is to be very serious, and to have no illusions."

When you fly to Milan, you will arrive at Malpensa Airport, 29 miles from the center of the city. A bus connects with the central railroad station. All over Milan, you will recognize the underground by its orange signs and the letters MM, Metropolitana Milanese. There are two lines, red and green, MM 1 and 2. You may buy tickets at the newsstand in the station, and stamp them at the turnstile before boarding the subway. You need exact change to use in ticket machines. Weekly passes require a photo, which you can take to the ticket office at the central station. Look for signs reading *vendita biglietti* (tickets sold) when you want to buy tickets. You can hail a cab in the street or go to a taxi stand and wait.

Servizio compresso on your restaurant tab means tip included, but as small change (called *spiccie*) is returned to you, leave this for your waiter as well.

Milan offers great shopping with frequent special sales. Its Quadrilatero area consists of four streets of elegant furs, jewels, antiques, and designer goods. A noted department store, Rinascente, offers un po' di tutto (a little bit of everything) for shoppers.

In Milan, there are reductions on clothing in different markets every day. Outside the city, you can find extraordinary designer goods at bargain rates. You will see designer eyewear (manufactured in northern Italy for Calvin Klein, Armani, Yves St. Laurent, Liz Claiborne), selling in America for up to $250, for a fraction of the price. At nearby markets are gloves, handbags, ties, scarves and woolens from the same workshops that produce for Gucci, Ferragamo, and Valentino, at incredibly low prices.

While you are in Milan, take in the spectacular, awe-inspiring view from the Duomo, the oldest Gothic cathedral in the world. Visit the celebrated Teatro alla Scala, one of the world's great opera houses, and see Leonardo's Last Supper in the Church of Santa Maria delle Grazie.

A male model who comes to Milan may take longer to start working, unless his reputation precedes him. Once he starts, however, he won't stop. Many male models stay in Milan for extended periods, and travel to other markets, including some of Italy's regional ones like Bari, Bologna, Ravenna, Ancona, Florence, and Verona, all of which offer plenty of work for men. Men find Italy is very sophisticated and fashion oriented.

Europe has an enormous designer business, and some men based in Milan pick up agencies not only in Paris, London and Germany, but also in Amsterdam, Vienna, Belgium, Greece, Spain, Scandinavia, and Portugal, and work every day of the year, six days a week. Some men are booked nearly a year in advance.

London

Foreign models with experience and good books can easily work in London. The market has excellent photographers and many high paying accounts; however, London is a tough city for the newer model, because clients prefer working with pros. Hamburg, Paris and Milan make more allowance for inexperience.

Full service agencies all have print, TV, and runway divisions. London agents will arrange work permits and explain things clearly to the new model. Rules are written in a book called "Terms, Conditions, and Standards for the Engagement of Professional Models in Still Photography."

Pay from clients in London is delayed three months. In the interim, the agency will advance 60% of the invoice, and later keep 15% in reserve, in case of problems. Their commission is 20% and there is a 5% fee for funds advanced.

Models are expected to be on time for appointments, and some agencies will take disciplinary measures if they receive complaints from clients. London agencies often find lodging for models, sometimes with families. If grooming is needed, models are sent to dance and exercise classes, to makeup artists and hairdressers.

British-born David Bosman, founder of Boss Models, says: "There's a definite beat that London is where it's at. All the ideas are coming out of Europe at the moment, and especially London, and it's exciting. People are looking for models with character, and that's what they think London models have."

London has more men's magazines than almost any other city in the world, David Bosman emphasizes, which helps create a strong market. "London is a melting pot, and there's a lot going on here." London makes room for men who are drop dead gorgeous as well as those with street looks; however, muscle-bound hunks are unacceptable, one reason being that they don't fit sample sizes. The London market is especially sensitive to male models who are acceptable to straight men as well as to women.

When you arrive at London's Heathrow Airport or at London Gatwick, follow the green sign if you have nothing to declare, the red sign if you have. The underground connects with all tube stations in London. To the center of town is a 45 minute trip. Or take the Airbus, doubledecker red bus, that goes into the city every 10 minutes, in which the trip takes 50 minutes. There is also a green coach bus service. Taxis charge extra for luggage. Daily, monthly and weekly tube passes are available at Victoria Station, with a photo required for the weekly and monthly passes. If a bus has "request" written on it, put out your hand to stop it. Cars drive on left side of the road, so look right before crossing.

While you're modeling in London, be sure to take in the changing of the guard at Buckingham Palace, Windsor castle, the ride down the Thames, the Tower of London, Harrods, Westminster Abbey, the British Museum, the Tate Gallery, the second hand stores at Portobello Market, West End theatre and Hyde Park.

Zurich

Zurich is not a city for beginners, but experienced models can make excellent money here. Zurich will pay promptly, some accounts even the same day you work, some on the 15th of the month. Catalog is an excellent market. Agency fees are 25-30%. About 75% of the models are American, valued for their professionalism.

Very few photographers are available for testing in Zurich, whereas a good portfolio and tear sheets are essential to work here. It is recommended that new models get a book and tear sheets in Milan, which is only a four hour train ride from Zurich. In fact, many models commute regularly between Milan and Zurich.

Be sure to come to Zurich with good accessories and makeup.

Japan

Tokyo and other parts of Japan are excellent markets. There are many fashion shows in April and May, perhaps 10 per day. Models can earn excellent deal of money in Japan. Tear sheets are good to have but not necessary. The pace is strenuous, demands high. Agencies charge a 20% commission and you must pay a 20% withholding tax as well. You must have a valid visa, for which you should go to the Japanese Embassy or Consulate in the US, with 3 passport photos, a letter on letterhead, two composites, and three professional photos or more.

Government law decrees an exclusive 60 day contract between the Japanese model agency and foreign models, which can be extended for another 60 days. Agencies must guarantee minimum earnings, whether the model works or not, must also give a pre-paid round trip airline ticket and provide living accommodations to the foreigner. Usually minimum guarantee contracts are worth several thousand dollars.

Models arriving in Japan are met at the Tokyo's Narita Airport by an agency representative. One of Tokyo's prime agencies keeps three dozen apartments for foreign models, all excellent accommodations, with living room, separate bedrooms for each model, kitchen, towels, sheets, western style furniture and daily maid service. A model can earn $1000, $1500 or more a day easily, and pay back their agency advance in a week's time. The agency also puts out money for composite mailings prior to the model's arrival. You will be paid at the end of the contract, but in the meantime, the agency will advance a living allowance.

Male models do well in Japan. The Japanese like men to be slim, good looking, and wear a size 40 regular suit. There is a great deal of work, and it's a big market for foreign male models. Female models need accessories and a good shoe wardrobe. Models are taken to on appointments in the agency staff car. Shopping in Tokyo is expensive.

On the streets of Tokyo you will encounter members of the Good Will Guide Program, 16,000 volunteers who wear purple and white badges for identification. They all speak foreign languages, mostly English, and are there to answer your questions and be helpful to tourists.

Guidelines For Models Abroad

When you go abroad to work, be more cautious than you would be at home until you become acclimated. You are on unfamiliar ground, so be on your guard at first. American girls can be especially vulnerable to exotic-sounding foreign accents. and courtly manners American girls often don't catch on when a fancied latin lover is just flirting, and mistakenly think he's in love. French and Italian men especially enjoy the game of love, the amusement and diversion of what Italians call *il flirt*, or *l'avventura*. If you receive an invitation to a man's apartment, avoid going unless you know what you're getting into, and are open to accept anything that happens.

One American model who asked her name be withheld fell in love with Italy, and adored the company of Italian men, whom she found to be so utterly charming that she was caught unawares. Once a good looking Italian man she was smitten with took her for a drive to his country villa near Lake Como, where he tied her to the bedpost and refused to return her to Milan for days. And that was just the beginning.

In many ways, Europeans grow up faster than Americans. Drinking is legal in Germany at 15, and it is unlikely anyone would object to serving a glass of wine or beer to a teenager in other European countries, either. German supermodel Claudia Schiffer was discovered dancing in a European discotheque at 15. The discovery of an American teenager in such a sophisticated ambiance at this tender an age is doubtful. Europeans are raised in an atmosphere that makes them more attuned in to the adult world and able to fit into a grownup lifestyle than are their American counterparts.

Most Europeans have been served small amounts of wine and beer with their meals since childhood, even as infants, whereas Americans have not, thus young American girls may not know how to handle alcohol. It is advisable for teenage models to avoid alcohol if for no other reason than appearance. Alcohol and drugs can affect the hair and skin, causing blemishes, puffiness and dullness. A model must pamper her physical appearance. Diet, sleep and exercise are important in order to maintain professional standards. Post-midnight nightclubbing can be a temptation, but modeling is a profession, and your reason for going abroad is to work, not play.

If you go abroad to model

– Know whom you are dealing with. Preferably work through a US agency who will sponsor your sojourn abroad.

– Don't drift idly from country to country, hoping to get work. Choose your base; settle there and dedicate yourself to success from that one central spot, then travel as job offers come in from other locations.

− Be sure to buy a return ticket before you leave the US, or know that your family can be relied upon to buy it for you if you need it.

− Don't travel with excessive cash.

− Have sufficient funds to survive till you start working -- which could be months.

− Read foreign magazines to see what look is in.

− Lose weight before you go, not when you arrive.

− Know your measurements in the metric system – centimeters and kilos.

− Understand the Euro currency.

− Do not give an agency wrong measurements.

− Health and accident insurance are important.

− Don't deal with strangers who claim they want you to work for them; insist they go through your agency. If you have a gut feeling something isn't right, trust your instincts; back off. Better safe than sorry.

Accept ahead of time that your initial experience abroad may be slow, riddled with rejection, or you may get lucky and start working almost immediately.

Take side trips. Become part of the life in another culture. Learn the language of your host country, and pick up other languages as well. Become more international in your outlook.

For international assignments, you may need the following basics and accessories

– Black and flesh colored underwear, strapless bras.

– Light and dark pumps, dressy evening shoes, sporty shoes, flats, sandals.

– Makeup, lipsticks, different color foundations and eyeshadows, eyeliner, mascara, nail polish (make sure it doesn't leak).

– Hair accessories and hairspray.

– Hot rollers, curling iron, dual voltage hairdryer, converter kits, travel iron.

– Jewelry, scarves, sweaters, hats, belts, gloves.

– Blouses, shirts, pants, suits, dresses, casual wear, formal wear, tights, sweats.

CHAPTER 11 - MODELING SCHOOLS, BEAUTY PAGEANTS, CONTESTS, SCOUNTS

One route to modeling may sometimes be through attending a modeling school, which provides preparation for what will be called for in a professional career. Other possible channels to a professional career include modeling contests, competitions, conventions, and beauty pageants.

Modeling Schools

A modeling school can be a way to start, particularly if you live far from a major market or are a beginner and need training in grooming and knowhow. The curriculum of a modeling school is usually of special interest to teenage girls, who love to experiment on their appearances and learn grooming tips. A modeling school adds polish.

Courses in the basics of posing, hair and makeup, wardrobe, fashion, acting for commercials, fashion photography and runway are offered in modeling schools. Most schools work with video, so you can see yourself on screen and learn from mistakes.
The curriculum will offer techniques in grooming, clothing and fashion, beauty, makeup, skin and hair care, nutrition, exercise, diet, and other important personal development areas. Some schools offer coaching in how to break into modeling, will help the new model get tests, and will make recommendations to agencies.

Pointers To Learn at a Modeling School

– What to put in your tote bag

– How to handle go sees

– Different modeling markets

– How to conduct yourself on a set

– How to read a script and do a cold reading

– Preparation for fashion shows, (conducted like a professional show with rehearsal time, lineup, run-throughs, etc.).

– TV commercial acting on video: reading scripts, videotaping, playback with class critique

– Rejection and how to handle feelings of insecurity.

Some schools and workshops offer a special photography package to cut expenditures that could otherwise add up fast. From some of these workshops the model comes away with a series of test shots, done at a special all-inclusive rate.

Well known former fashion model Heather Cole runs model camps in Virginia, New York, Los Angeles, Miami and Toronto for girls ages 7 through 18. Nearly 5000 young women have passed through Heather's portals. A native of Britain, Heather initiated her own international modeling career in New York, working for such clients as *Vogue, Harper's Bazaar, Marie-Claire* and *Elle*, modeling all over the world for eight years before settling down outside Washington, D.C., and opening her Model Source Agency, followed by her Cole's Model Camp/Modeling Development. Heather's goal is for all girls to realize their inner beauty and to leave the programs with a stronger sense of self-esteem. Heather's curriculum emphasizes personal grooming, fashion design, and modeling etiquette.

For those interested in careers in fashion design and photography, Heather also runs a sister program, Camp Fashion Design, with help from "Project Runway" winner Lisa Nargi and "America's Next Top Model" winner Ashley Howard.

At Jo's International Models, Inc., Training Center for Models in Florida, "Personal development is an ongoing transformation, an experience that we want to keep foremost in our lives. Without it, we are less than we can be." Jo teaches a 10 week charm course and a 12 week modeling course: the 10 week program emphasizes personal development, poise, posture, positive attitude, self confidence, beauty, mannerisms, grace, makeup/hair secrets and more.

In the 12 week modeling course Jo delves into modeling etiquette, runway techniques, photography secrets, national vs. foreign markets, interviewing styles, go sees, your portfolio, and much more.

Besides classes, Jo offers individual workshops for runway training, photography and makeup. Classes at Jo's are tailored for ages 4 and up.

Page Parkes, Houston, Dallas, and Miami, offers a modeling school, Model Camp, beauty seminars, children's seminars, and other teaching facilities: Page Parkes Center of Modeling develops potential talent by offering professional training classes to prepare one with tools necessary to begin a career in commercial print and acting.

Page Parkes says, "A first rate modeling course will train you in hair and makeup techniques, give you a complete makeover and hair cut, teach you the basics of runway, photo posing, commercial print, provide you with a professional portfolio, give you tools to succeed in the business."

But Page also cautions the hopeful model: "Be sure you are dealing with an established, reputable school that has the connections to place you in a reputable agency once your training is complete."

Page recommends models check the status and credibility of a school or agency by calling local department stores and ad agencies, the Better Business Bureau, and well known model agencies east and west cost. Ask if they work with or have information about a particular agency or school; find out how many years the company has been in business -- with the same owner. Check with the State Licensing Board to see if the agency or school is certified and/or regulated by the State. And be wary of any company that guarantees you a job – a sure red flag.

Summers, Page Parkes Center of Modeling hosts a 2-day International Agent Review seminar in Houston, where models and actors meet with agents from New York, Miami, Dallas, Paris, Milan, Japan, San Francisco, Atlanta, Australia Spain, Chicago and Los Angeles. Here, hopefuls learn from industry's top pros – photographers, stylists, hairdressers and makeup artists; agency images the model head to toe, conducts a runway and/or acting workshop; one-day Agent Review Prep and photo shoot includes information to help a model make a great impression; photo shoot to update composite and portfolio; team of fashion, hair and makeup stylists and photographers shoot three complete looks.

"Some of the best models in the world come from neighborhoods just like yours!" says the brochure heralding Page Parkes' Model Camp. Camps are offered several times a year in Dallas, Houston, and Miami, where small town aspirants can learn the business inside out from the experts – award winning photographers, makeup artists, and fashion stylists – who teach insider tricks and help develop the model's portfolio. Extensive workshops in makeup, wardrobe, and movement help models become at ease under the lights, ready for professional assignments.

Page Parkes' Model Camp workshops have taken beginners and made them working models overnight.

Beauty Pageants:

Local beauty pageants, state fairs, and beauty competitions are held all over the country, most of them on a regular annual basis. These may be judged by professionals in the modeling field, who will sometimes sit down with contestants and advise them how to get to the next step of a career. In some instances, if deemed unsuitable, the candidates are advised not to pursue modeling. You can find beauty pageants and their requirements listed online.

Contests

Modeling contests are held all over the world, some of them of several days' duration. Some give out cash prizes and other compensations. The most lavish end in grand finale banquets where hundreds of prizes are awarded. Frequently, half a dozen or more of the 1000 entrants are offered recruitment contracts with top New York agencies. Some contests announce winners in several different categories: high fashion, junior, commercial, male models, and other.

Some contests provide the winner with an all expense trip to Europe, a new wardrobe, and a location booking, stylist included, testing with one or more photographers, and other perks. The model can come home with prints that make a great portfolio, and also meet top international agents via this method.

Two of the most famous annual contests are Ford's Supermodel of the World and Elite's Look of the Year.

Modeling schools may also hold contests and award prizes.

Modeling Conventions

At least a dozen different groups hold conventions, many of which last three days to a week, at which hopeful models have an opportunity to discuss career possibilities with the experts – casting directors, agents, established models and other guests. Formats consist of competitions, workshops, seminars, open interviews, callbacks, panel discussions and various other events. Some of the more elaborate conventions employ a specialized technical crew for showcase productions and fashion shows.

International modeling conventions are held in several foreign countries as well as in the United States. One of the best known of these conventions are those produced by IMTA, or International Modeling and Talent Association, of Phoenix, Arizona, which holds its world famous week-long conventions twice yearly in Hollywood and New York.

At IMTA, models and talent compete in runway, print, TV and other competitions, and seminars are conducted by experts in beauty, fashion, modeling, acting, singing, and dancing. More than 1000 beautiful and talented men, women and children throughout the United States (including Puerto Rico), Mexico and Canada come to meet over 200 top agents and casting directors from around the world – from every major market in the US, along with Paris, Milan, London, Hamburg, Madrid, Athens, Tokyo, and Brazil – who participate as judges and scouts. Auditions and agent interviews are held, with many contracts signed. Trophies, cash prizes, and scholarships are awarded.

Models and actors who gained their first big exposure from an IMTA convention can be seen on the covers and in editorial pages of leading fashion magazines worldwide, in TV commercials, soaps, sitcoms, and films.

Says Helen Rogers, the lovely ex-model who is founder and President of IMTA: "IMTA is unsurpassed in bringing to the forefront an incredible diversity of beautiful faces and talented performers who join the stars of fashion, film, television, videos, commercials and theatre... Fashion and entertainment history is ... made as the stars of tomorrow are discovered at IMTA."

Helen Rogers is one of the best known people in the modeling and talent business. Helen's own career as a model began with the Ford Agency in New York, where she modeled for three years, appeared on many covers (including Mademoiselle), and was photographed by the top fashion photographers in the business.

Helen moved to Los Angeles, continuing her career in print and TV commercials. After transferring to Phoenix, Helen became ABC's weather girl and hostess on a game show before opening her first modeling school and agency, Flair, which became an instant success. Two of her students were among the five winners in Vogue magazine's model contest. With the Phoenix market growing rapidly, Helen opened the prestigious Plaza Three modeling school and agency, whose models were scouted by all the fashion capitals of the world.

IMTA conventions are recommended by Ford Models, Elite Model Management, The Savage Model and Talent Agency; Click Models, Why Not Agency, Milan; Visage, Osaka; and many other top agencies around the globe.

"A once of a lifetime opportunity for prospective models to be seen by international agents," says Lynn Claxon, Stars The Agency, San Francisco;

And says Sawako Saito, Ad Plan, Tokyo: "I would describe IMTA as simply Subarashi!" (Japanese for fantastic.)

Conferences

Delia, of Delia Model Management in Wilmington, North Carolina, runs a modeling conference twice a year "which is very different from the big conventions, in that I only take very young models, up to age 25; although ours is very small, lots of success has come from it."

Delia, who hails originally from London, has found some great models at her conferences. "So I am very proud of that," Delia says, "and I'm always looking for the `new star.' I have a couple of girls right now, one 13, the other 15, that I think have the potential to move in that direction."

Are Modeling Schools on the Up and Up?

The major criticism of modeling schools is that they may give false hopes to candidates unqualified for modeling. Delia says, "I started – quite frankly – because I was upset with the `modeling schools.' I am not saying all are bad, but to take in a 5'3 inch girl who is overweight and promise her she can be a model, or give her a `graduation certificate' is wrong. I struggled but only took girls that I felt strongly had potential, which was hard to do."

There are legitimate modeling schools out there who evaluate a model's chances honestly and do not mislead, Delia emphasizes. Best are the schools that offer a curriculum that is primarily geared to personal improvement, and make no promises that girls can become models.

Delia has this to say about small town modeling: "People need to know that not all small town modeling development agencies and schools are bad."

Modeling Scouts

Worldwide, scouts are on the prowl looking for young people with something special, that one in a thousand who can earn big dollars as a successful model. Scouts attend contests, visit schools and pageants, and in addition to approaching models, are approached by them in turn as well. Some scouts will talk to aspirants on an individual basis to give advice.

What are scouts looking for? "An extroverted, compelling personality," says one scout. "Quirkiness," says another. "A strong face, versatility," says yet another. "Someone with an unusual quality – beauty and ease in front of the camera."

Through whatever channel you arrive at modeling, your job will be the same: you must work on yourself, expose yourself, constantly reinvent yourself, promote and sell yourself.

CHAPTER 12 - ADVICE TO MODELS

Modeling do's and don'ts:

A model should avoid overexposure in any one market, and work in more than one area to increase chances of a substantial income. Never ask for allowances or special dispensations, and never offer excuses. You are there to do a job and to be the consummate professional; your career depends not only on your physical attributes but on your performance, your manners and your professionalism.

You must always seek to discover new facets within yourself, and aim to always improve by being self-critical of yourself. Remember that a model must always be up, even when she's down.

On Handling Money

A good portion of assuring your future is learning how to manage money wisely. Learn good money management. Take courses on the subject, watch financial programs on TV, subscribe to financial newsletters, and by all means, make sure you have a good accountant.

The Taxman Cometh - A Model's Deductible Business Expenses

– Photos, prints, composites, comp cards, headshots, glossies, photo duplication and other lab work, retouching; portfolios, mini-portfolios; agency fee for book and other agency promotional materials, post cards, greeting cards and other mailings, advertising and publicity.

– Makeup and other cosmetics, facials and other beauty

treatments; waxing; dermatology, plastic surgery, skincare.

– Hair, hair coloring and salon treatments; trichologists, hair products and accessories.

– Manicures, pedicures.

– Dental bills

– Body conditioning, health club membership, exercise class, equipment and wardrobe.

– Professional wardrobe of costumes, expanded wardrobe, business wardrobe.

– Lessons, acting, dancing, voice, music, etc.

– Smartphone, tablet, fax, computer and related products, hardware, software

– Transportation, buses, subways, airlines, boat, hydrofoil, car mileage, tolls, taxis, travel around town and out of town.

– Videos, voice tapes, demos

– Workshops, seminars, contests and pageants

– Books, magazines, trade publications, fashion and other publications, newsletters, foreign publications, records, tapes.

– Union dues

– Letterheads, supplies, postage, printing and design

– Travel and Entertainment

– Gifts

– Tailoring and cleaning

– Agency commissions and other commissions.

– Professional fees (accountant, lawyer, financial advisor), etc.

– Singing, dancing, acting lessons, fencing, etc.

– Spas, special diets

– Other medical; health insurance

– Umbrella policy

Keep written records of all transactions and appointments. Record expenses and billings. Retain all receipts. Better yet, scan them into your computer. Use smartphone apps to keep track of your expenditures, so many of which will be deductible on your income taxes.

Keep in mind

Get a good night's sleep before bookings, always be well groomed from head to toe, be on time, never become impatient with repetition, and never quit or attempt to quit a job early. Stay away from arguments – it doesn't matter if you're right because the client is always right. Let your agency handle controversial or unpleasant issues.

The more you audition, the more polished you become. Remember that many models are after the same job, and that a client's decision has nothing to do with you as a talent. Promote yourself; never stop promoting, and be ready to go in any direction the door opens.

Constantly seek to improve your physical presentation: posture, mannerisms, expressions, voice, diction, how you stand, walk, sit; your body language.
Take exercise and dance classes – ballet, tap, jazz; voice, speech, acting, commercial, modeling and self improvement classes.

Lessons, workshops and seminars should be an ongoing part of your self-improvement.

– The camera adds weight – maybe as much as 10 pounds – so keep your weight down.

– If you lack inbred grace and style, set about acquiring them. Make refinements in the way you walk and talk, in your vocabulary and mentality.

– Don't slouch. Keep a tall line when you sit, keep your head up.

– Learn to project confidence and always strive to maximize your presentation.

– Observe other models and copy the best of the best.

– Do away with distracting mannerisms.

– "Smile!" (Christie Brinkley, when asked what it takes to be a good model).

– Learn to be the consummate professional.

Projections for the Future

In modeling, you should always be thinking about the future, about what you want to be doing in three months, six months from now, a year, two, five, ten years and more. You need to always be setting goals, otherwise, you may end up with a limited career. Setting goals includes not only short term modeling, but goals for a life after modeling, perhaps using modeling as the entré to a related career, as so many successful models have done.

Remember that personality can be 50% or more of your success, and that models are booked according to how well people like them as well as how good they are. Those in a position to hire like having a pleasant person around.

Modeling takes perseverance and dedication, but those who pursue their career with this at the forefront of their mind will see rewards. Modeling today is wide open; never before have so many opportunities been available. The multi-billion dollar fashion industry alone has grown by leaps and bounds. Added to that, new vistas for the male supermodel, jobs in television commercials, and other areas proliferate.

In a profession that has more job insecurity than most, modeling entails a perpetual search for work. The truth is that models never truly arrive – or at least they don't think so – and are ever in search of more, greater, better, the next job, the higher level. Models are always looking for what's coming next. Those at the top are forever creating and recreating, inventing themselves anew. If you want to be a model, you will either have this inborn aptitude to grow and recreate yourself, or you will learn it along the way.

Make the most of these years afforded you to solidify the opportunities modeling has brought, and make the right moves. With your success, acknowledge how lucky you are to be a part in the most competitive yet gratifying business in the world. And at the same time, be aware of others' contributions, knowing that without them you could never be where you are. Your collaborators – agents, bookers, photographers, hairdressers, wardrobe and makeup artists, editors, casting and advertising people, directors, clients – each plays an important part in your career, and each one prides himself/herself on the role they play in your life. Allow them to bask in your success and enjoy the satisfaction they too have earned.

True gratitude is always appreciated by others. You are truly blessed to have the qualities giving you the opportunity to be a model. Never forget how privileged you are, and always express your thanks to the many people along the way, without whose help you could not have become who you are.

Godspeed!

XXXXXX

MODELING GLOSSARY

Action: A call by the director that cameras are ready to begin filming a scene.

Ad: "Advertising" or "advertisement."

Advance: Up front money, to later be deducted from earnings.

Advertising agency: Company hired to promote product or service.

AEA: Abbreviation for Actors' Equity Association, union for stage actors.

AFTRA: Abbreviation for American Federation of Television and Radio Artists, performers' union, now combined with Screen Actors Guild (SAG) as SAG-AHTRA.

Age range: Age span within which a model or performer appears usually 4-7 years.

Agency: Representative who sends models on job calls, negotiates rates, contracts and handles models' bookings.

Assignment: Booking, modeling job.

Audition: Tryout in which models and talent are chosen.

Beauty shot: Headshot with main focus on face and hair.

Book: (a) Noun designating model's portfolio; (b) verb meaning to hire a model for a modeling job.

Booker: Model agency employee who schedules appointments and handles models' assignments.

Booking: Job, assignment.

Booking out: Activity of model when he/she will be unavailable, so that agency will not book him/her at that time.

Budget: Amount of money needed or available for a specific purpose.

Buyout: One time payment in lieu of residuals or royalties, which entitles client to unlimited usage of a photo or commercial.

Callback: Second, third or more audition, usually used in commercials.

Casting: Process in selecting a suitable model. In the US, used as a verb, usually in connection with commercial, stage, TV, and film work; in London, "casting" is used as a noun, interchangeably with go see, interview, and audition.

Casting director: Works either independently or in house; screens talent for final interviews and auditions for jobs.

Cattle call: Mass interview, in which scores of models/talent are interviewed for a job.

Catwalk - Runway

Celebrity model: Film star, sports or society figure or other well known person who endorses or pitches products.

Checker: At fashion show, person who makes sure models are correctly dressed and placed.

Class A, B, C commercial: Union method of calculating residual payments, based on number of cities a commercial runs in.

Client: Person or company retaining models' services, such as advertising agency, manufacturer, designer, catalog, magazine, etc.

Closed set: A set on which only those directly involved are permitted (such as cast and crew); requested when discretion is advised, such as in the filming of a nude scene.

Cold reading: Spontaneous reading of script without previous rehearsal time.

Collection: Designer-made samples or originals, shown to the public.

Commercial: Television or internet advertisement for a specific product.

Commission: Sum agency deducts from models' earnings for their services, usually 20% (plus 20% from the client).

Competition: Other models who are trying for the same job.

Composite: Mass produced photos showing a model in different styles, moods, angles, etc., containing measurements; handed out to prospective clients by model and/or agency.

Conflict: A product or service competing with another, forbidding models from appearing in rival product.

Contact sheet: Proof sheet, displaying exposures in small format.

Credits: Jobs a model has done.

Crew: Technical group behind the scenes: director, assistant director, makeup, hairstylist, wardrobe, electricians, grips, prop people, camera operator, lighting director, etc.

CU: Closeup

Day rate: Model's fee for single booking for a full day.

Director: Person in charge of the set in film or tape shoot.

Dolly: Equipment used for tracking shot.

Dressers: People assisting models backstage during live fashion show.

Dubbing: Substituting one voice for another, often from one language to another.

ECU: Extreme closeup.

Editorial print: Magazine pages produced by staff rather than advertisers.

Exclusive: Model may work for one particular client only during a given period, may not conflict with other bookings.

Exposure: Visibility in media.

Fashion model: Model with correct qualifications (size, age range, etc.) who models clothing in magazine editorial, runway etc.

Fashion show: Presentation collections, ready to wear, sportswear, etc. of specific group of clothes.

Fashionista: A person of taste and with great fashion sense who ardently follows the fashion scene.

Feature film: Full length motion picture for theatrical, broadcast televison, or cable release.

Fee: Amount of money model charges for services.

Fitting: Session in which model tries on clothing prior to wearing it in a booking.

Flat fee or Flat rate: One time payment, similar to buyout.

Gaffer: Electrician, moves lights and other equipment in film production.

Garment district: Area of city in which apparel showrooms are located.

Glossy: Mass produced 8 x 10 photo, to which resume is usually attached.

Go-see: Interview to secure work.

Grip: Crew member, moves cameras and sets in TV and film production.

Hairdresser, Hairstylist, or hair designer: Cuts, sets, and styles models' hair.

Headsheet: Large sheet or brochure showing photo reproductions of models an agency represents.

Honeywagon: Mobile lavatory used on location shooting.

House model: Models who show clothing at designer's showroom.

Industrial film: Film made to educate, entertain or instruct.

Informal modeling: In which model strolls through an ambiance such as tearoom, restaurant, country club, mixing with customers while showing garments.

In the can: Footage already shot from a script.

Junior model: Model who wears sizes 1-9; is not as tall as high fashion model; looks younger than high fashion model.

Large size model: Also called plus size, wears size 12 or up.

Lighting: Arrangement of lights for a particular scene.

Lingerie: Intimate apparel jobs.

Live promotion: In person modeling at trade shows, stores, etc. to demonstrate or promote products and services.

Location: Place other than studio where job is photographed

Look see: Calling on client, so client can look at model and model's book.

Loupe: Magnifier to view slides, contact sheets.

Madison Avenue: Advertising agency district in Manhattan.

Major market: Major US market is New York; major European markets are Paris, Milan, London.

Makeup artist: Specializing in application of makeup.

Market Week: Time of the year when apparel is shown, buyers come to the garment areas to place orders.

Marks: Designated spot for model to stand.

Mini-portfolio: Small duplicate of model portfolio sent to prospective clients, also called mini-book.

Model release: Form signed by model giving photographer or client the right to sell or publish pictures from an assignment.

On camera principal(s): Main character(s) in a project.

Overscale: In film or television, a higher payment than that established by SAG-AFTRA.

Overtime: Work that lasts longer than the normal 8 hour day, or work that occurs on a weekend or holiday.

Parts Modeling: Hands, feet, legs, etc.

Penalty: Charged in special circumstances: (a) when a shooting does not allow for proper mealtime breaks or violates other union regulations; (b) when model must make a change in appearance that will inhibit future earnings, etc.

Petite model: Junior size model

Plus Model: Large size model.

Portfolio: Model's book of photos and tear sheets.

Pose: Stance, position in front of camera for shoot.

Presser: Person responsible for ironing clothes that are being modeled in a show.

Principal(s): On camera key figure(s) in commercial or other shoot.

Print: Still photography work, such as editorial print, advertising print, etc.

Producer: Oversees entire production in film or tape shoot.

Product demonstration: Showing how product works; usually done live.

Proof sheet: Contact sheet, proofs.

Property person, prop man: Responsible for props used on set.

Public relations: Publicity.

P.R.: Abbreviation for public relations.

Rag trade: Garment industry, (aka the schmatte trade).

Rate: Model's fee. May be an established rate; a negotiated rate or a client mandated rate.

Reading: Audition.

Release: Contractual agreement between client and model, spelling out terms, authorizing use of model's image.

Reshoot: If first try is unsuccessful, job must be reshot.

Residuals: Fees paid in commercial usage.

Resume: List of credits, experience, vital statistics, union affiliations, special talents, attached to back of composite or glossy.

Rounds: Seeing a series of clients in a position to employ the model..

Runthrough: Rehearsal prior to performance.

Runway: Area on which models show clothes in fashion show; also called a catwalk.

Rushes (dailies): Footage viewed by director and selected others from previous day's shooting.

SAG: Screen Actors Guild, union now combined with AFTRA (American Federation of Television and Radio Artists), known as SAG-AFTRA.

Scale: Minimum money performer may charge in film or videotape, determined by the union.

Schmatte trade: Garment industry, rag trade.

Script: Written copy containing dialog and actions to be executed on camera.

Script supervisor: Oversees each take, makes sure shots match.

Sed Card: Also called comp card, Z card (Zed card.

Shoe model: Sample shoe size, usually size 4, 5 or 6 for a woman, 10 for male model.

Show modeling: Live presentation, fashion show, runway, etc.

Showing collections: Live presentation of designer styles held in Milan, Paris, London, New York, Tokyo.

Showroom: Designer salon in which clothes are shown to buyers.

Showroom model: Shows garments to buyers in designer's or manufacturer's showroom.

Sitting: Shooting.

Slating: Identifying film or videotape take, scene, etc.

Slides: Processed 35 mm film, encased in plastic.

Sound person, sound man: Handles sound recording in film, video.

Spec: Payment upon acceptance.

Spokesperson: Individual representing a product or service, endorser doing a direct pitch.

Spread: Featuring several photos in two or more pages devoted to a single concept or model.

Starter: Responsible for seeing that models appear on the runway on time.

Storyboard: Drawings and text showing how a shoot will be executed..

Stylist: Assists photographer and editor, selects accessories, props, to be shown with garments, supervises shoot, making sure clothes are in good order.

Take: Shooting (and recording) of a scene in filming or taping, Many takes may be required before the desired effect is obtained. Each take is slated for future reference.

Talent: Model or actor who performs in filming or taping.

Talent agent: Represents talent, sends them out on go sees and interviews.

Tearsheets: Pages from magazine, catalog, or other printed material showing model's work.

Trade show: Show held in a convention center or hotel for a specific product category: auto show, boat show, computer show, flower show, etc.

Trunk show: Fashion show featuring designer garments traveling to various cities, usually held in stores.

Typecasting: Assignment of roles based on appearance.

Union card: Card designating the person is a member in good standing of a specific union. In many cases, talent may not work without a union card.

Usage fees: Additional fees paid when the model's image and likeness is exposed in additional markets.

Voiceover: Job or lines performed off-camera.

Voucher: An invoice documenting a job has been completed.

Wardrobe: Garments worn by model in a booking; may be owned by model or client.

Weather permit: Job dependent on favorable weather conditions.

#######

ABOUT THE AUTHOR

Jeanne Rejaunier graduated from Vassar College, and did postgraduate studies in Paris, Florence, Rome, and at UCLA. While a student at Vassar, she began a career as a professional model, and subsequently became an actress in Manhattan, Hollywood and Europe, appearing on and off Broadway, in films and television, on magazine covers internationally and as the principal in dozens of network television commercials.

Rejaunier's TV commercial credits include: Coca Cola, RCA, Revlon, Yuban, Mennen After Shave, Noxzema, Pond's, Buick, Arpege, Ivory Liquid, Zest. Pepsodent, Chesterfields, United States Navy, Aquaduct Race Track, Clorox, Bryl Creme, Cutex, Ballantine, and numerous others. In Hollywood and in Europe, she appeared in several motion pictures and in television series.

Rejaunier achieved international success with the publication of her first novel, **THE BEAUTY TRAP**, which sold over one million copies and became Simon and Schuster's fourth best seller of the year, the film rights to which were purchased outright by Avco-Embassy. Rejaunier has publicized her books in national and international tours on three continents in five languages. Her writing has been extolled in feature stories in *Life, Playboy, Mademoiselle, BusinessWeek, Fashion Weekly, Women's Wear, W, American Homemaker, Parade, Let's Live, Marie-Claire, Epoca, Tempo, Sogno, Cine-Tipo, Stern, Hola, The New York Times, The Los Angeles Times, The Washington Post*, and countless other publications.

In addition to **THE BEAUTY TRAP**, Rejaunier commercially published two other novels, **THE MOTION AND THE ACT** and **AFFAIR IN ROME**, as well as nonfiction titles **THE VIDEO JUNGLE, ASTROLOGY AND YOUR SEX LIFE, ASTROLOGY FOR LOVERS, JAPAN'S HIDDEN FACE, THE COMPLETE IDIOT'S GUIDE TO FOOD ALLERGY**, and **THE COMPLETE IDIOT'S GUIDE TO MIGRAINES AND OTHER HEADACHES**.

Branching out as a filmmaker, Rejaunier produced, directed, filmed, and edited the four hour documentary, **THE SPIRIT OF '56: MEETINGS WITH REMARKABLE WOMEN**.

######

THE BEAUTY TRAP, by JEANNE REJAUNIER

"Here is a novel that can't miss, crammed with all the ingredients that make a blockbuster." - **Publishers Weekly**

"A startling closeup of the world's most glamorous business, an intensely human story." - **The New York Times**

"Jeanne Rejaunier has concocted a sexpourri of life among the mannequins that's spiked with all the ingredients of a blockbuster bestseller."- **Playboy**

"A fascinating inside story of the most glamorous girls in the business, absorbing to read." - **California Stylist**

"This is Miss Rejaunier's first novel. We can't wait for her second." – **Tampa Tribune**

"New York's most sought after women find themselves having to make desperate decisions that will affect their very lives." - **Wilmington (DE) News Journal**.

"The novel is rich in esoteric commercial lore about modeling...." **Saturday Review**

"She packs a no hold's barred picture of the New York fashion scene. Sales of the book are approaching a million copies in the United States." - **London Daily Express**

"Possibly the most honest novel to appear by a female writer in the past decade."- **Literary Times**

"Miss Rejaunier is most interesting when she goes behind the scenes in the modeling world." - **Detroit Free Press**

######

36567547R00103

Made in the USA
Lexington, KY
27 October 2014